CULTURE AND POLITICS

D1617182

Culture and Politics / Politics and Culture

General Editors:
Laura Nader, *University of California, Berkeley*
Rik Pinxten, *Ghent University*
Ellen Preckler, *Ghent University*

Cultural Identity, whether real or imagined, has become an important marker of societal differentiation. This series focuses on the interplay of politics and culture and offers a forum for analysis and discussion of such key issues as multiculturalism, racism and human rights.

Volume 1
Europe's New Racism: Causes, Manifestations and Solutions
Edited by **The Evens Foundation**

Volume 2
Culture and Politics: Identity and Conflict in a Multicultural World
Edited by **Rik Pinxten, Ghislain Verstraete** and **Chia Longman**

CULTURE AND POLITICS
Identity and Conflict
in a Multicultural World

Edited by
Rik Pinxten, Ghislain Verstraete and Chia Longman

Berghahn Books
New York • Oxford

First published in 2004 by

Berghahn Books
www.BerghahnBooks.com

© 2004 Rik Pinxten, Ghislain Verstraete and Chia Longman

Library of Congress Cataloging-in-Publication Data
Culture and politics: identity and conflict in a multicultural world / edited by
Rik Pinxten, Ghislain Verstraete and Chia Longman.
    p. cm.
Includes bibliographical references and index.
ISBN 1-57181-334-9 (alk. paper)
1. Politics and culture. 2. National characteristics. I. Pinxten, Rik. II. Verstraete,
Ghislain. III. Longman, Chia.

JA75.7.C8563 2004
306.2--dc22

                                                                    2003063913

British Library Cataloguing in Publication Data
A catalogue record for this book is available from the British Library.

Printed in the United States on acid-free paper.

ISBN 1-57181-334-9 (hardback)

Contents

Preface

In the heart of the research group 'Centre for Intercultural Communication and Interaction' (CICI) at Ghent University, Belgium, we have been discussing the texts in this volume for the past two years. The research group is a semi-loose context of research and debate about culture, interculturalism and fundamentalisms in the present era. Some of us are full-time researchers (L. Orye, C. Longman and A. van Dienderen), while others have staff positions (R. Pinxten, K. De Munter) and still others have a position in applied research (G. Verstraete). The group is nonetheless substantially larger than the set of contributors to this volume (we count some fourteen regular members in the meetings of CICI, while over the years seven more researchers have been hired by the Centre on a temporary basis).

After contributing as a group to several international conferences (the meetings of the European Association for Social Anthropology of 1998 and of 2000, for instance), we decided in 2000 to engage in a book project, which would deal with a few of the central issues with which our individual researchers are concerned: cultural identity and cultural differences, and political discourse on culture and otherness. A former joint publication in Dutch (Pinxten and Verstraete 1998) would serve as a primary source of inspiration in view of a clarification of the notion of identity which is subscribed to in CICI as a whole. At the same time, we wanted to respect the personal foci and the field specialisms of each of the individual contributors. The result of this exercise is the present volume.

Without doubt there are common grounds or shared notions in the chapters in this book. However, they do not stand as immutable guiding principles, let alone as dictates for any of the authors in particular. First of all, we do not believe such a doctrinal approach to research is workable, let alone desirable. No mastermind or supreme authority is at work in CICI, and none is to be expected in this volume. Furthermore, we think that the subject matter which we are studying exemplifies that uniformity is a mere fiction but one with political appeal, alas. It would be self-contradictory to strive for uniformity in a strict sense in a group that documents the enormous diversity and the dynamic nature of the identity phenomenon to begin with. Finally, the research group is an interdisciplinary group. Although we are concerned with the same or very similar topics within CICI, there is no disciplinary unity. This was and is a deliberate choice, since we all feel that the social and cultural world we are dealing with is so diverse that an interdisciplinary approach stands a better chance of reaching relevant insights than a disciplinarily constrained focus. Since our primary audience is that of anthropologists, we figure this is not really a handicap.

Given all this, we still claim some unity in our diversity. First of all, we all share a deep interest in the concept of identity and we all believe it more appropriate to speak of 'identity dynamics'. We share the insight that present debates pertaining to identity are often profoundly ideological, both within the scientific disciplines concerned and in the sociopolitical context we live in. In the introductory chapter, we invite the reader to appreciate this aspect and we offer an analytical framework that will help the researcher to move beyond any ideological dichotomy and hence reclaim the notions of identity for scientific research. The reader will appreciate that Lieve Orye (Chapter 1) carries through a parallel analysis in the field of religious studies, where scholars struggle with a deep-seated bias in understanding the religious realm, which shows a similar dichotomisation and investment in ideological identity notions. In yet another field of study, namely gender studies, Chia Longman (Chapter 2) finds strikingly similar lines in her work on religious identity among strictly Orthodox Jewish women. Both authors investigate the ways the basic notions in their research fields can be exposed as ideological constructs, in order to reclaim them as scientific concepts of analysis subsequently.

In a second move, the introduction stresses that identity dynamics are not a mere academic subject. Scholars in this type of field potentially have political impact, and, therefore, it is important to be as clear and as explicit as possible. After having analysed and reformulated questions of identity, it is necessary to reclaim political stands. Koen De Munter (Chapter 3) focuses primarily on this aspect in his study of the impact of identity dynamics in the political reality of non-Western groups, such as the Aymara Indians of Bolivia today. An van Dienderen (Chapter 4), finally, gives a detailed analysis of the way nonverbal formats and carriers of meaning, such as pictorial representations, determine and impact identity dynamics in their particular ways. She does this by analysing the picture on the cover of this volume by way of example, thus ending the book with an analysis of the meaning of the cover in its silent conveyance of a thread of unity throughout the diversity of the book.

We hope that the book will provoke discussion on the topics treated, especially regarding the concern we share among ourselves, and offer to the reader ideas on the ways we can combine science and ideology in culture-laden fields.

Rik Pinxten
Ghislain Verstraete
Chia Longman

Bibliography

Pinxten, Rik and Verstraete, Ghislain, eds. 1998. *Cultuur en macht* (Culture and Power). Antwerp: Hadewych.

INTRODUCTION

Rik Pinxten and Ghislain Verstraete

Introduction

In the past decade we have been working out a comprehensive analytical frame-work on identity and conflict. It distinguishes three levels of extension (the individual, the group, the community), where identity is construed in terms of personality, sociality and culturality dimensions. The model is deliberately nonessentialist, dynamic and multifaceted. It has been applied in the description of some cases around the world (France, Belgium, Siberia, Kivu-Rwanda, Bolivia, etc.) in Pinxten and Verstraete (1998). We argue that an analytical framework is needed which can serve as an instrument that will allow us to speak with scientific rigour about the various dimensions of identity.

The present chapter in particular focuses on the notion of culturality and its relevance as 'one dimension of identity dynamics'. It is obvious that the notion of culturality has a markedly different and indeed more restricted meaning here than that of culture in most anthropological studies. This position needs defence and explanation. We propose this particular notion of culture (i.e., the culturality dimension) deliberately and consciously in a context where 'culture' increasingly appears to be replacing 'race' within the discourse of the extreme right in Europe. Hence, introducing a notion of culturality in identity discussions is a politically relevant move. Such a move is argued both on the basis of scientific rationality and on the basis of political choices. An example from the field of studies of our centre will illustrate the argument.

On Reclaiming Identity

We see ourselves as living in the situation of Otto Neurath's sailors. In his famous metaphor about knowledge, Neurath states that the continuous rebuilding and reshaping of knowledge can be viewed very much like the rebuilding of a ship while it is sailing the high seas (Neurath in Cohen 1964).

In the present contribution we are very conscious of this predicament: it is impossible to 'step out' of the world of social, cultural and political forces and structures in order to reshape it and finally to implement the result of our thoughts into reality. As anthropologists (or social scientists in a more general perspective) we are fully aware that our thoughts and analyses may impact the sociopolitical reality we are examining. One of the intentions of this chapter is to invite the reader to look at the possible frames of the 'ship' of social and cultural identity, firstly by studying its plans.

For decades, anthropologists have been struggling with two supposedly opposed traditions of scientific work, implying quite different understandings of social and cultural phenomena. Illustrative is E. Service's (1989) overview of one hundred years of anthropology under the appropriate title *A Century of Controversy*. According to Service's analysis the Durkheimian, positivistic and sometimes scientistic approach can be identified as one school of thought in Western anthropology. The focus hereby is on 'social facts' of any type, while 'culture' is seen as – at the most – a rather unimportant by-product or residue of the social world. The alternative view, then again, is held by the so-called culturalists, who have tried to identify a layer of 'super organic' reality. Early on, figures like F. Boas were classified as culturalists, and via C. Lévi-Strauss the present-day interpretive anthropologists (starting with Geertz 1973) are also often characterised as culturalists or philosophical idealists. In a very recent attempt to think through the basic concepts of cultural anthropology, Borofsky et al. (2001) invited distinguished scholars in the field to re-address the issue of sociologism versus culturalism in order to determine what notion of culture would be a scientifically tenable one. Since American anthropology overwhelmingly focuses on the notion of culture (in comparison with the British or the French schools, for example), the exercise is a significant one. The results are indicative of the point we are trying to make here: some authors claim that one does not need the vague notion of culture if one sticks to a solid sociological analysis (e.g., Barth in Borofsky 2001), while others side with the culturalists (e.g., Shweder, ibid.). Our point is that scholars are trapped in prescientific positions, endlessly elaborated on in further work, but whose fundamental value is never questioned.

As scientists we need to look for some kind of yardstick which would enable us to appreciate the relevance of the analytical terms of culture and social reality, rather than keeping us trapped in mere ideological positions like culturalism and sociologism. Only then will the seemingly mutually exclusive 'theories' appear as alternative perspectives on the 'ship' we are sailing, not different 'ships' all together. In other words, we reject the obligation to choose on a priori grounds for either a sociologistic or a culturalist position, but rather wish to search for a scientific criterion which will make both appear as particular foci on the complex reality we are studying. Our analytical framework of dimensions of identity will serve the purpose of the yardstick here. A by-product of this type of approach is that the essentialism lurking in some of the present identity claims can be identified and critically assessed for what it is, namely an ideological construct. To phrase it even more explicitly: the ship can be viewed from both the perspective of the culturalist and from that of the sociologist, but we should refrain from seeing the ship as either a 'cultural ship' or a 'social ship'. For, in the latter case, we would have started out from one or the other a priori. Such a detached view is necessary, since it will enable a deconstruction of the dichotomy of culturalism versus sociologism as an ideological one. It will subsequently allow for a reconstruction of both perspectives as heuristic paradigms, to be tested on their own worth.

In order to make this shift from an ideological (and somewhat ontological) view on identity towards a scientific one (in terms of perspectives) we claim that two particular lines of questioning are most valuable: first, we state that the essentialism in the sociologistic and in the culturalist positions is an uncalled-for addition which does not stand in the light of serious scientific critique. Secondly, we hold that most of the time human beings are demonstrably engaging in communication, interaction and/or negotiation in their sociocultural life. Hence, essentialism in the guise of culturalism (e.g., in the new rightist parties) or of sociologism (e.g., in the laicist French position) is then an extreme and basically exclusive form of communication, which can be labelled 'monologual', rather than dialogical or interactive. In our view essentialism does not belong in the realm of social reality, but is a particular and rather closed view of groups and individuals on socio-cultural life. Hence, it is an ideological position, which can be recognised as such, but does not qualify as an analytical tool of scientific research.

Culture and Identity

What we are aiming at in this volume is to deconstruct these notions and the way the relationship between them is often defined. In doing this, we reclaim identity as a scientific term (especially in Orye and in Longman) and as a political term (see De Munter and van Dienderen). This work is precarious, since we have to do it in the political contexts and the power-ridden situations in which we live.

An Appetiser

In a small city (of 40,000 inhabitants) in the vicinity of Antwerp we asked a self-identified spokesperson of the Moroccan community to arrange for us to meet with some young people in order to interview them for a research project concerning parent participation in schools. We looked for subjects who (a) were considered to be successful by the community, (b) were aged between twenty and thirty and (c) were raised and still lived in the city. Our questions centred on factors which had enhanced their success in school. The following picture emerged:

1. Intelligence and tenacity in schoolwork.
2. Character to decide with whom and how to spend leisure time.
3. Early 'maturity' to study autonomously, with clear goals.
4. A school with a good class, forming a social network.

5. A family with older brothers and sisters who aimed at good school results.
6. The fact that one's family would not belong to one of the two larger clans of the Moroccan community in the city. Hence, one could be free of an avalanche of mutual visits and festivities which abound within these two clans.
7. A certain degree of freedom vis-à-vis conservative/religious/traditional parents. This kind of freedom is only possible away from the environment of the clans, allowing for self-determinacy.

Looking at the list of factors which was given across the board by our interviewees, it appears that personal issues are identified next to social and so-called cultural issues: 4 and 6 are more social, but 5 and 7 seem to be 'cultural' elements. All of the factors are felt to be crucial for their identity by the youth. What approach in anthropology or social sciences could do justice to this list of identity markers? Some theories would focus on the personality aspects (1–3) and hence draw a psychological picture, while other ones would focus primarily on the social and psychological issues, emphasising the family ties. There seems to be nothing specifically 'Moroccan' here, whereas focusing on the 'otherness' of the youth would overemphasise the cultural issues.

This example shows what we want to investigate and why we need a strong and efficient instrument to do that, beyond the disciplinary models which are available at present. Rather than choosing to interpret the reality we confronted in the a priori frame of the culturalist or that of the sociologist, we wish to problematise these a priori positions.

The Instrument

In this section of the chapter we recapitulate the work we have done so far. In our struggle with the vague notion of 'culture' in its new prominent role beyond anthropology and into the political discourse of today, we develop an encompassing analytical framework which should enable us to get a grip on the multifaceted domain where 'culture' is claimed to be relevant. One major stumbling block, we claim, is the often downright essentialist discourse on 'culture': anthropologists of the past and political analysts of the present refer to 'culture' as an entity or as a fixed and core element of a (large) group. In the anthropological discipline one speaks about 'a culture' and defines the world's population as consisting of some 4,000 cultures (e.g., in the standard reference system of the Human Relations Area Files, started by Murdock and others: see Naroll 1983). In the past, the advantage seemed to be that one could point to structural characteristics, which could be distinguished from the next culture, having its own particularities. On closer examination, however, it proved to be next to impossible to stick with any classification, let alone to deal with continuous processes of change (because of war, exchange or trade, cultural traits are continuously transported, altered or abandoned by groups). Is a Chinese person becoming less Chinese and more of a Western cultural subject by eating a hamburger? Or is Western culture lost because of Chinese restaurants which are to be found on practically every street corner, or the African music which is part of the world of experience of today's Western youth? There is no way to use this culture-as-entity notion in a clear and scientifically proper way, we believe.

The other common usage of 'culture' points to a set of basic characteristics that is adopted by a population, and that is hence considered as a deep value or a core of the survival system which marks that population as somehow distinctly different from the next one. Basically, the same sorts of problems are attached to this notion as to the previous one. Yet this has not prevented some advocates from making 'culture' into the main identity factor of a population, or its motivational force in intercultural conflicts. At least some of the prevailing theories on nationalism and on major war threats defend this point of view (alternating 'culture' and 'civilisation' on some occasions: e.g., Huntington 1996). It is even worth while to look at the UN peace treaty over Bosnia in this respect. The academic debate on the issue is then often narrowed down to one between so-called culturalists and others.

In our view this sort of approach is blind to a set of other factors that seem to be at play in so-called intercultural conflicts, whilst it still works with an encompassing but definitely unworkable category of 'culture'. Instead, we propose to capture the field in a multilayered and multifaceted approach to identity, conceptualised as a complex of ongoing processes. We propose the term 'identity dynamics' in referring to the field of phenomena at hand. With this conceptual move identity is reclaimed as a scientific term. The conceptual framework developed below will allow us to test identity dynamics with scientific rigour. In making this move the ideological usage of the concept of identity in present social scientific discourse is rejected. In this volume Lieve Orye (Chapter 1) develops a parallel analysis in the realm of religious studies. She shows that scholars in that field are trapped into a similar choice between two ideological positions: one is supposed to take a religionistic or a reductionist stand on religion. The appropriateness of the concept and the term of religion as a scientific or analytical category is her point of discussion.

Identity dynamics are held to be characteristic, in a nontrivial way, of processes of growth, decay and change in the self-image and the interaction potentialities of individuals, groups and communities. These are the three levels of extension we differentiate in the human social arena, as they are distinguished from one another by a formal criterion: the set of interactional relationships of each is intrinsically different. An individual can interact with him-/herself in a way that is indeed qualitatively different from the type of interactions s/he can have with other individuals or sets of them. The interaction to oneself is reflexive. However, no individual exists in isolation: the individual interacts through interpersonal relations with others, thus relating oneself to one or more groups. Hence, the second level of extension, the group(s), can be defined intrinsically as any set of individuals with real interpersonal or face-to-face interaction. Each individual belongs, most of the time, to more than one group: an alliance group (e.g., a couple), a family, a professional circle, a ceremonial group, and so on. At the level of highest extension we define communities as those sets of people who interact, so to speak, in a virtual way: one cannot have face-to-face contact with 'the New Yorkers' or with one's ancestors. But it is clear that 'New York' or a 'clan' can be very important in identity conflicts all the same.

At each of these levels identity dynamics are at work. We distinguish between three sets of constitutive features, called 'dimensions'. They are differentially working at each level, depending on the traditions or learning strategies of individuals, groups and communities. The dimensions are:

1. *Personality* Here we refer to personality studies in psychology (e.g., intelligent, beautiful, introvert, etc.), but also social psychology and sociology (conformist, leader, etc.) and anthropology (e.g., Dionysian versus Apollonian personality in Ruth Benedict's model). In all social sciences personality has been studied, using various philosophical a priori (e.g., psychoanalytic versus system theoretic stands). It must be granted that the psychological personality studies of Western subjects are the most elaborate for the time being, but the study of personality is not the sole prerogative of the psychologies of the Western individual, as more or less extensive sociological and anthropological theories of personality have shown (Roland 1991).
2. *Sociality* 'Sociality' is characterised as a multitude of transpersonal sets, constituted by means of convictions, rules and learning procedures which detail how, when and under what conditions persons, groups and communities interact and communicate. We rightly say that individuals are socialised, that is to say that they learn how to behave with other persons, or otherwise relate to others in different ways by descent, alliances, and so on. Regulations on gender, descent, marriage, neighbouring, etc. belong here.
3. *Culturality* We define 'culturality' as the dimension which comprises all those processes which 'produce meaning'. The understanding of meaning we advocate is that of meaning in context, which thus involves situating the processes in their sociohistorical and political settings. Obviously, meanings are instrumental in identity dynamics in a differential way: sometimes, but not always, for this individual or community, but not for that other group, etc. Since 'culturality' is only reserved for the meaning-producing processes of identity in this contribution, it will never be an encompassing dimension, but rather one of the set of three dimensions. We are aware that meaning production in identity dynamics is a very strong emphasis in the Western (Christian) tradition, bestowing meaning on almost everything having to do with identity at all three levels, but we claim this is a typical feature of that complex of identity dynamics which we call 'Western' and which could be tracked down to a fundamental feature of Christianity. It does not necessarily have the same span of application to all human interactions. Thus, it should be possible to speak about ritual education in Hindu tradition as a basically meaningless socialisation process (Staal 1988), whereas a puberty socialisation process in Western-Christian groups will be invested with meaning. In the scientific approach of a decolonised social science, we should allow for a set of concepts that see the prevailing Western social scientific concepts as special cases and not as universal or technical categories.

The relationship between sociality and culturality in this approach can be seen as analogous to (with the risk that every such analogy holds) that between syntax and semantics-pragmatics in linguistics. Although the linguistic relationship is a difficult one too, it is conventionally agreed that syntax and semantics-pragmatics refer to different aspects of language (notwithstanding their close relationships and often intermingling in actual performances). The interplay between syntax and semantics-pragmatics makes a linguistic message into a communicable utterance, but both syntax and semantics-pragmatics have a semi-autonomy which can be studied in its own terms. We can teach syntax by educating children in the rules of a language so that they will be able to form grammatically correct and communicable utterances in that language, and we can teach about meaning-in-context of a language by learning such intricacies as polysemy or metaphor. Some aspects can be purely or basically grammatical (like word order), while others are identified as primarily concerning meaning (like double meanings in a joke). The analogy we are using here can be formulated as a homology: it stipulates that sociality stands to culturality in identity dynamics like syntax stands to semantics-pragmatics in language (including language learning).

An example will make this clear: in their synthesis of the field of ethnocentrism studies LeVine and Campbell (1972) present a list of some twenty-four characteristics ascribed to 'us' (and their counterparts attached to 'them'). Thus, 'we' are seen as morally good and hence we are the subject of love by our peers, while 'they' are regarded as morally bad and hence they rightly are the subject of our hatred. In the view of the authors the synthesis yields a universal model of ethnocentrism, using the twenty-odd features to compose identities of an in-group and of out-groups. When working in the field with Navajo Indians one of us grew conscious that although Navajos are markedly ethnocentric, the model does not apply. They would classify all others as non-Navajo/enemies by birth. However, this does not imply that non-Navajos should be hated, or that Navajos should be loved and appreciated as superior to the 'others'. The construction of us–them distinctions is by no means absent, but at the same time it did not correspond at all with the contrast features of LeVine and Campbell's model (Pinxten 1997). Our interpretation of this finding is that the 'syntactic' distinction us–them applies also among Navajo Indians (expressed in sociality categories which distinguish between groups and group adherence along these lines), but that the 'semantic-pragmatic' categories varied substantially. That is to say, the cultural identification of the Navajo us–them distinction is very different from the Western one. Thus, LeVine and Campbell's synthesis remains very valuable, but we claim that it only deals with Western culturality in ethnocentrism.

We distinguish between two vehicles for identity construction and marking at each level: narratives and labels. Through narratives an individual, a group or a community secures integration over time. That is, the constant manifestation of identities in ever-changing contexts is accompanied by narratives which enable the actor to position and reposition him-/herself. Thus, conflicts between former and present actions can be smoothed by an accompanying narrative. In the second place, all individuals, groups or communities identify themselves and/or are identified by others by means of labels (such as signs, uniforms, particular words or a specific tongue, etc.). Especially in the development and the management of conflicts, narratives and labels can work as important vehicles indicating escalation or de-escalation of conflict: e.g., shifting to warlike language and codes, rewriting one's history during and after a conflict, and so on. Again, although narratives and labels cannot be seen in themselves as the nucleus of a conflict, they are indicative and offer relevant entries for studying the conflict. Of course, other aspects need to be attended to as well, such as material context, power balance and so on.

When we combine the levels and the dimensions, the field or domain of identity dynamics is characterised in the following model:

1. *Individual identity dynamics* are constituted and reorganised constantly by changing values on three parameters or dimensions:
   • personality: the physical and psychological make-up of each individual: strong, shy, emotional, beautiful, intelligent, masculine/feminine, young/old, etc.
   • sociality: the forms and means to fit into transpersonal settings: sociable versus individualistic, integrated versus displaced, etc.
   • culturality: the meaningful aspects in individual identity: a conscientious individual in the Christian religiopolitical tradition, a responsible capitalist in the present-day West versus a redistributive leader in Tuareg civilisation before the emergence of the new states, etc.
2. *Group identity dynamics:* group identities are constituted and continuously rearranged along the following three dimensions:
   • personality: certain professional groups may require a particular personality type (e.g., salesmen should not be shy, cheerleaders should be young, etc.), while others will induce a particular mixture of personality types (e.g., the staff of a university department). Other groups may be indifferent to personality characteristics (e.g., age classes for puberty rites).
   • sociality: the 'grammar' of a group can be very specific (e.g., initiated males only, that is, only those males who know how to behave in the select group of village elders). The rules and habits of interaction in a hierarchical family are quite different (implying heritage agreements, respect, etc.) from those of a leisure group of cyclists.
   • culturality: e.g., the historical references of a family (with a genealogical tree, a religious belonging and an economic tradition) bestow different meanings on the group's identity than the revolutionary vocation of a group of partisans who fought for the freedom of their city in Ghent, Flanders during the Second World War.
3. *Community identity dynamics:* again the three dimensions are constitutive:
   • personality: communities can select for, educate towards and allow special room for particular personality types. For example, Rambo and Marilyn Monroe are considered to be role models for the Westerner at the end of the second millennium, whereas they are seen as handicapped 'half-persons' (lacking feminine and masculine aspects, respectively) by Navajo Indians.

The research into so-called national characters illustrates how personality types can be constitutive for the identity of communities: e.g., the male-dominant, conformist and collectivist Saudi as opposed to the feminine, creative and individualistic Swede (e.g., Hofstede 1993).

- sociality: different communities socialise their members in a different way, rearing them in a different set of structures and mechanisms. Thus, the social contract model prevails in the West, whereas kinship-based power for the elderly is the rule in traditional rural communities.
- culturality: particular meaning-producing processes can operate on the level of communities. The processes will vary vastly at this level: e.g., the Christian tradition gives meaning to life and death and pervades the moral and political sphere profoundly in Western societies; the community bestows meaning through textual historical references, through interiorisation of good and bad by means of generalised education, and by organising life in terms of punishment and reward at every level (including jurisdiction). The Navajo community, on the other hand, attaches meaning through contextualised oral referencing (in myths and ceremonials), through rearing its members in a guilt-free control system, and through procedures to seek compensation and balance in conflicts rather than deciding who is 'right' and who is 'wrong' according to some preestablished written rule. The difference in meaning giving can be vast: an almost encompassing meaning system prevails in the religious communities around the Mediterranean, whereas 'local' meanings seem to leave room to realms devoid of meaning in other communities.

An Example: Reactions in France to the Gulf War of 1990

On 2 August 1990 Iraq invaded Kuwait. The same day the UN Security Council votes a resolution condemning the attack as an act of aggression and demanding immediate withdrawal of the Iraqi troops. From then until the end of November no less than ten resolutions are voted. Also, an embargo is declared against the state of Iraq, enforced from the sea and from the air. On 17 January 1991 a coalition led by the U.S., starts the Gulf War. The war is brought 'live' on television all over the world, broadcast from aboard the bombers. The war escalates when Iraq successfully hits Israel with Scud rockets. France sends 19,000 soldiers, 14 ships, 500 tanks, 120 helicopters and 60 aeroplane bombers.

The ensuing public debate in France is centred mostly on internal affairs: the main fear is that Algerian immigrants and the 'pieds noirs' in France will get into conflict with the Jewish community there. By the end of January, hundreds of thousands of 'Islamists' are protesting in Algiers, demanding that the Algerian government train Islamic volunteers to participate in the war on the Iraqi side. Spokesmen say on French and Belgian television that this war is only an excuse for the West (and mainly the U.S.) to further establish world hegemony by crushing Islamic regimes. The Palestinian case is discussed as the real issue of this war. In the south of France civilians are seen to buy more arms than usual and in some cities they even start bunkering supplies. At the same time church leaders, university professors and politicians speak up to keep the public calm. On 22 January and 4 February representatives of the Catholic Church, the Protestant Church and the mosque of Paris issue joint statements to 'live by the spirit of fraternity of the children of Abraham' and to avoid confrontation amongst each other. In most cases such appeals, also by state officials, are directed towards the communities of origin. The citizens from Maghreb origins, often those born in France, express their concern with this approach: they feel they are 'taken into hostage' by the French state's singling them out and addressing them as 'Arabs', rather than as Frenchmen. Thus, the state shifts in identity attribution in this matter and focuses on Arab, Christian and Jewish identities rather than on national identity for its own citizens. Some citizens take this issue up and declare they feel 'aggression against our origins' (as Muslim, etc.) by this overseas war of France and their American allies. Others express their disillusion in France, and declare themselves incapable of identifying with 'those people' (i.e., French officials).

But the war is not only an issue in public debate. In daily practices and interactions shifts in identity are experienced as well. Individuals and groups are sensitive to changes in context[1] and express shifts and changes in their identities. We give some examples from the interviews carried out in France (Schnapper 1993; translation ours):

A 30-year-old educational aid worker from Maghreb origin, but born in France, stated: 'I was behaving like any other young person; I was drinking alcohol. But suddenly, from one day to the next I was scolded to be a filthy Arab. Before that event, I was never thought of as an Arab. I was indifferent to the issue, since I was with French colleagues. I was with young people, and that was it. There are people who do not feel attached to communities, and even reject them. But all of a sudden you become an "Arab".'

A 33-year-old university staff member from Algerian descent told us in one of the interviews we carried out: 'Not anti-racism, but racism became normal. Even some shopkeepers refused our money. At that time I had some trouble with a grocer about a silly matter, a mere futility. I had peed against the wall of her house. She ran outside and started scolding me. She demanded to see my ID and said: "In this city there are some 5,000 followers of the Front National now. After the next elections we will certainly count 10,000 and then we will come and get you." The police picked me up and brought me to their station.'

A 57-year-old Jewish woman told us: 'In the beginning I was lost. I felt a deep solidarity with the Jewish people... But at the same time I wanted to know more about Islam. I gained information and urged friends to do as much. Now many of them did not take this for granted.'

So, in daily practice and in concrete contexts of work, friendship or family, shifts appear. Not all of them need to point in the same direction. In the first example the labels were changed and the individual was thereby moved to another level of identity: the group level of colleagues at work is left for the community level of 'Arabs'. In the second example the emphasis is on norms, rules and constraints of socially acceptable behaviour. In the mind of the shop-keeper the misbehaviour has to be punished, and hence she takes the stand of community representatives in power and threatens the individual in the name of the community. In the third example, an individual who identifies herself with a community first and foremost, starts searching for meanings that would transcend the community level of identity and is reprimanded for it by the community.

Thus, the international conflict poses a series of internal problems in France because it is lived and understood in a set of different identity processes by the subjects and the state. The official 'Western' identity discourse proclaiming that the war has to be fought because of the violation of human rights, as the basis of UN actions, is part of the identity narratives of next to none of the citizen groups and therefore constitutes yet another narrative at the international level. It is questionable whether it unites the West, let alone the world. The resurgence of the Front Islamique de Salut (Islamic Blessed Front) and the Groupements Islamiques Armés (Armed Islamic Groups) in Islamic countries may be taken as an expression of quite a different reading of contextual and of intrinsic aspects of this international conflict in yet different identity terms. It is our conviction that such an example can show which different sets of dynamics are at work in such conflicts, using quite diverse and often oppositional labels and narratives. In the following months the conflicts in France grew and frustrations vis-à-vis the state may be difficult or even impossible to ease for years to come.

This example does not deny that 'real' military and economic interests and conflicts were at work in this case, but it aims to show that people's identity dynamics can also operate as causal forces in the development and treatment of such conflicts. This inspires us to describe them as distinctly intercultural con-flicts because they are significantly codetermined in their origin or phasic development by culturality features as well. Moreover, the shifts and changes in and by the conflict of identity constellations justify our dynamic approach. (The actual historic developments in France are further documented in Ver-straete and Pinxten 1998.)

Culture or Culturality

In treating this subject for a readership of anthropologists, politicologists and sociologists we need to go deeper into the issue of culturality. As we mentioned earlier, a strong current in European and American anthropology is culturalist in one sense or another, understanding 'culture' as the pivotal element on which groups or communities differ from each other. The history of the concept of culture, however, is a bleak one: notwithstanding the efforts of hundreds of researchers in this field, no definition was ever agreed on by any representative sample in the discipline.

Our move in this chapter and elsewhere is double: on the one hand, we want to resituate the cultural phenomenon, and, on the other hand, we aim at fighting the unhealthy essentialism we encounter. A very similar line of thinking is developed in this volume by Chia Longman (Chapter 2). She analyses the debate on identity from the perspective of gender sensitivity. In the particular domain of gender identity she scrutinises the essentialism which is hidden in the dominant conceptual frameworks and proposes ways to adopt anti-essentialist stands.

The essentialist use of culture is most clearly expressed in the common reference to 'a culture', identifying a community which is somehow distinctively characterised by a set of features that are not biological, and are hence termed cultural. In the century-old debate between social and cultural anthropologists (Service 1989) the culturalists have been stressing that groups or communities differ transgenerationally and/or structurally by their cultural features, often at the expense of (social) scientific methodology. The difficulties in reaching a scientifically sound model or concept of culture (as a culture) are plenty: it is impossible to demarcate a culture because of borrowing, war and trade which continuously change the picture. Also, it proves impossible to identify a culture as a diachronic and hence changing phenomenon, leading to the denial of a historical dimension to non-Western communities (Fabian 1984). These two criticisms may be the most important ones (though not the only ones: we should include orientalism and other bias thresholds in the picture) inspiring our decision to drop the concept of a culture altogether. We speak about material units instead: persons, groups and communities, distinguishing between all three by means of intrinsic features of the interactions of each type of unit. What was and is studied under the name of 'culture' is seen as a part of the complex of processes of individuals, groups and communities, a complex we call identity dynamics. Only those features and phenomena which somehow or other involve the production and transfer of meaning are dealt with in the category of dimension of culturality. The first major problem with the old concepts of culture is thus dealt with: the essentialism is avoided.

In the example we used above it became clear that the presumed national culture of France was threatened by the culturality aspects of different groups and communities in France, who stressed their particular identities over and above that of their national identity. A comprehensive and marvellously detailed picture of the multicultural political landscape of modern France is to be found in Pierre Bourdieu's (1994) book on the old and the new poor in the cities.

A second problem remains, however. Why do we still require the concept of culturality, and what does it stand for? Why not do away with the cultural, as some materialists or social anthropologists do? Our model leaves room for culturality as the dimension which deals with contextual meaning-producing processes. We explicitly and expressly make room for such a dimension because we are impressed by the human capacity to invent, interpret, fantasise and symbolise aspects of the world. Neither a purely materialist (e.g., Harris), nor any formal approach (e.g., Chomsky) so far has offered an adequate theory of these human capacities, we claim. Hence, any reductionism which denies meaning a place next to syntax seems unwarranted. This meets the challenge we set ourselves: avoid the trap of essentialism, but also that of reductionism, by exposing both as ideological positions. The model will allow us to cover the subject matter and test the viability of the perspectives we advance.

Since we want to construct a comparative model, the category of meaning-producing processes is kept as open as possible: that is to say, it would involve phenomena which can either be found under semantics (reference, meaning, even deixis) or pragmatics (use, speech act meaning), as well as nonverbal or paralinguistic meaning (as in proxemics and the like). Moreover, we explicitly state that the contextuality of interactions and communications are included in the notion, leaving room for the particular contextualisations each person, group or community recognises and uses. Although the notion of culturality may still be rather vague, its open-endedness is important for our purpose. Again, the example helps to illustrate this point: as stated, the Iraqi conflict was lived in very different ways by citizens of France, who often attached diverging or conflicting meanings to signs and acts in the process. The counterexample of the mere lack of a genuine public discussion on the topic in another Western nation adds to our consciousness of the impact of culturality over and above 'realistic' political issues (on the reception in the U.S., see Pinxten 1998). On this subject we share the view on conflict resolution and culture, which has repeatedly been expressed by the political anthropologist Robert Rubinstein (e.g., 2002): 'Realpolitik' misses the point by blinding us for culturally sensitive issues. In particular, the present post-Cold War era might illustrate the danger of this blindness, according to this author.

We grant that these are vast issues which need much more elaborate discussion than we can manage here. However, the approach we advocate may have been made sufficiently clear by now. Since we need a model that can describe in a comparative way markedly different processes of recognising and mapping personality, sociality and culturality dimensions, the present open-ended approach may do the job.

A final point needs to be made here. We consider the tradition in the social sciences and the humanities that withdraws into monocausality struggles as severely limiting: one explains the complex phenomena we are dealing with in terms of the algebra of underlying structures only (and hence becomes a convinced structuralist), or one accuses the former of idealism and resorts to a hardboiled materialism only (and thus becomes Marxist or conservative ecologist), or one takes one single other perspective as the rock bottom of an alternative theory. We are convinced that a scientific theory on such complex matters as social and political units and their histories will certainly be of a probabilistic nature (as natural scientists have grown accustomed to in the study of the simpler phenomena they deal with), and that complexes may have to be dealt with in a multitude of ways when looking for a comparative theory. We therefore shy away from simplistic monocausal explanations for the complex and dynamic phenomena we are dealing with and invite scholars from different perspectives to consider the present multifaceted and open-ended approach. It is our conviction that any choice for one or a combination of (probable) causes-within-a-context will emerge only after undertaking this exercise, if at all.

Dynamics, Change and Creativity

When dealing with issues like culture, change, tradition and so on, we are confronted with a host of attached problems. Partly, terminological questions interfere: for example, the connotation of stability and even unchangeability is still attached to the notion of tradition. Partly, we are in the midst of conceptual vagueness and die-hard colonial attitudes, when Western identities are thought of as more easily adaptable to new demands and hence in a sense more 'rational'. In view of all this, it is necessary to focus on such issues and make clear how the present approach wants to avoid such connotations and unwarranted colonial by-products.

It is our claim that any individual, group and community changes and creates (new, adapted) identities. Depending on intrinsic elements and on specific contexts this will happen at particular intervals, at particular levels of impact and with particular effects. With the present model we offer a means to recognise and conceptualise such changes along a variety of criteria and not along the criteria of one partner only. Looking back at the model, we predict that any momentary identity constellation is a mixture of values on the personality, sociality and culturality parameters at one time. But the mixture is somewhat specific for each agent. Some agents (e.g., the Navajo community after the Second World War) will keep talking about the Navajo way or about tradition by stressing a certain formal way of dealing with the world, almost regardless of the contents or of the meanings attached. This is somewhat awkward for the Westerner who particularly emphasises meaning and ideological or world view stands, and finds him-/herself at a loss when confronted with the seemingly meaningless or at the least indifferent Navajo way. Thus, it is perfectly possible for the Navajo community to integrate or Navajo-ise foreign elements in a coherent way, although these elements seem to conflict qua contents or meaning with each other. In fact, tradition in the Navajo way may well best be understood as precisely this coherent way of 'sucking up' and turning into aspects of one's identity anything useful or interesting, almost regardless of consistency in meaning (see Farella 1984; also Pinxten and Farrer 1993 on the role of paradox).

We think we can understand this by pointing to the larger range of the sociality parameter in such creative processes, compensated by a smaller range of relevant points for the culturality parameter, that is, larger and smaller in comparison with the opposite case along these lines, i.e., the Westerner. In Western identity processes we witness a very heavy emphasis on meaning production (and explanation) and a sort of horror for sociality devoid of meaning.

In anthropology there are examples which describe the processes and procedures of change, creativity and adaptation with emphasis on particular mixtures of the three parameters (personality, sociality, culturality). A great emphasis on personality (not disregarding the other parameters, though) will be found, for example, in revitalisation movements, religious movements and the like (e.g., Chief Wovoka's movement). A particularly prominent role of change along the sociality parameter was the focus of the Manchester school, with major contributions in the field of political anthropology by Max Gluckman and Victor Turner. Actually, the identification of ritual structure as a more or less 'syntactic' locus of change (i.e., sociality in our understanding) has been a major idea of Turner (e.g., 1969). In the present volume the contributions by Koen De Munter (Chapter 3) and An van Dienderen (Chapter 4) give ethnographic support for this idea.

De Munter carries out ethnographic work in Bolivia, where the Aymara redefine and relive their identity in the context of a metropolis like La Paz. The native intuitions on the dimensions of sociality and culturality are expressed in narratives and labels, which underscore the Aymara city-identity of today. An van Dienderen, on the other hand, offers a detailed analysis of the processes of identity formation in nontextual and nonliterate media. The analysis is substantiated by a description of the cover illustration of this book as the instantiation of one particular point.

Thus, to put it in a nutshell and oversimplifying for the sake of the argument, we claim that all agents change and create, but they do it in a variety of ways either emphasising sociality rather than culturality in one case (e.g., Navajo), or the culturality at the expense of the personality dimension (e.g., in religion-dominated societies) or the personality parameter at the expense of both others in a third case (maybe in the individualistic postmodern world).

Political Impact: Identity and Conflicts

Reclaiming identity is not only a matter of developing an analytical framework in order to allow for a scientific study of the issues at hand. By the very nature of the subject matter, it also has political implications. In the context of the West, ever since the fall of the Berlin Wall and the implosion of the USSR, choosing for one or the other perspective or model inadvertently draws the researcher into a political debate. Indeed, since that time the success of polemical and exclusive extreme right movements and political parties in the West has been such that the scientist's results are likely to be misappropriated in political debates. In particular, the scientifically nonsensical but politically successful use of culture and cultural differences as a line of propaganda by extreme rightists in elections throughout the EU should be a concern to scholars in this field (Evens Foundation 2002).

Anthropologists and sociologists are not often directly involved in political conflicts, but we recognise that the claim of rightist groups to draw on cultural origins, the discourse by native groups about cultural heritage, and the urgent debate on multiculturalism in the large nation states (U.S., Russia, but also the EU) forces us to confront the political implications of cultural issues head on. All of a sudden it proves unavoidable for the social scientist to take a conscious stand on political choices, although various 'postmodernist' predicaments may seem to have us locked away in a stuffy corner of academia. It appears to us that the reality 'beyond the text' is demolishing this fiction at high speed and is forcing us to understand that science and politics inevitably meet in our disciplines. Preston (1998) makes a plea for 'political/cultural identity' research in politicology. From the perspective of anthropology we can meet the politicologists in this project and offer what methods and insights we have developed in our discipline.

We distinguish between three problems here:

1. Culturality rather than culture allows for both a politically conscious and scientifically valid model.
2. Culturality plays an important role in identity dynamics and thus has relevance for conflict resolution involving identity claims.
3. Sustainable conflict resolution will most likely be reached by taking into account culturality aspects of all parties involved. To that end an intercultural negotiation procedure (with a comparative perspective) may be a necessary alternative to the monocultural negotiation models diplomacy has applied so far.

1. As mentioned before, the very notion of culture is scientifically indeterminable. At the same time it has recently been politically abused. Indeed, present-day political discourse in the EU uses culture and cultural differences at best in a very shallow way (not bothering about what would be cultural and what might be social aspects, for example), at worst as a catch-all term. The latter is exemplified by extreme rightists, who install an essentialist notion of the 'Other' as unalterably other vis-à-vis 'Us'. From this premise follows that coexistence, 'by the nature of the essences involved', is made impossible or at least very troublesome. The rightist think-tank GRECE in France thus picked up a reasoned suggestion about thresholds of identity by Lévi-Strauss (1973) and turned it upside down by claiming that we are doomed to be flooded and even annihilated by the Other coming here when we omit to stress our own essentialist identity as an insurmountable threshold at all times. In our own research on developing trajectories for refugees and immigrants in Belgium, we experienced how deeply rooted such biases are both among lay people and in policymaking circles (Verstraete et al. 2000). On the other hand, we think it cannot be denied that different contexts and their interpretation systems codetermine the identity complexes and the conflicts they play a role in. Therefore, we strive for an operational concept which to some extent covers the vague field and at the same time overcomes the handicaps of the anthropological notion of culture: we capture this concept under the label 'culturality', which is one of the three constitutive dimensions of identity processes of material units (individuals, groups and communities).
2. Culturality aspects (as values of one dimension of identity dynamics) play a differential role in identity processes: we think it unlikely that only one factor in the complex phenomenon of identity processes is the cause of all behaviour, beliefs, and the like. Our model provides for a diversity of factors at all levels: three dimensions together constitute the identity dynamics; identities are construed by and for three types of agents (individuals, groups, communities) all the time; any of the agents mentioned collaborates with,

opposes or is otherwise linked to a multitude of others (e.g., as an individual you are also member of a family, a clan, a nation, etc.); and personality, sociality and culturality values change over time and differ from context to context. This complex of factors can form a configuration which then triggers conflict with a similar complex from another person, group or community. We do not deny that one cause or reason for the conflict could be material needs (because of scarcity of goods) or power and territory interests. What we claim is that human beings, groups and communities enter into conflicts with their full human set-up, that is to say with the highly particular identity configuration which co-constitutes the agent. In that perspective it is possible to understand why people are willing to die for their country, or for their religion, or for their family in some contexts, and why in other places and times they may seem oblivious to demagogic appeals. The identity complex is at work here. Hence, identity dynamics with culturality aspects as constitutive elements have a political impact. Localising culturality as one dimension of what is politically relevant adds significantly to the potential of conflict analysis, and avoids the pitfall of the notion of culture as a reification of a super-organic entity, somehow over and above material agents.

3. In a scientific analysis a crucial aspect of the work is, apart from the conceptualisation of the problem, that of operationalising a basic insight. We opt for qualitative research, yet where necessary in combination with quantitative analyses. Anthropological fieldwork is an integral part of the empirical studies we advocate, without for that matter falling for the naïve fallacy that 'what the native says is always right'. On the other hand, the identity discourses of the subjects should be known by the researcher and the parties involved in a conflict and/or negotiation process, since here they are politically relevant. So in the concrete cases studied in our research group we document the histories, the narratives and the contextual data of the parties involved and explore their potential relationships.

Conclusions

In this chapter we developed a line of reasoning that would allow the researcher in the field of (cultural) identity to reclaim the term of identity as a scientific term. We feel that the debate is most often voiced in ideological categories, implying that the researcher has to choose a sociologistic or a culturalist stand on moral or ideological grounds. The dichotomisation of the field is, we claim, without ground. We have developed an instrument of analysis which can be used to investigate the problem area in a scientific way first, capable of exposing the unwarranted nature of the essentialist conceptualisation of identity. Our analytical framework approaches the field by looking for three distinct dimensions of identity dynamics: personality, sociality and culturality dimensions.

Having done this, we demonstrated how the analytical framework can be used to describe the multifaceted phenomenon of identity dynamics. However, in a second move we turn around and state that, because of the political weight of 'identity' in the present era, it is necessary to deliberate about political positions in the debate in the real world. Indeed, scientific data and models do not exist in a vacuum, but they are contrived and used in the very political contexts in which the scientist is working.

Notes

1. By context we mean a range of phenomena: practices and interactions take place in a physical context (time, space, material surroundings) and they belong to a realm of activities (work, family, professional activities). Moreover, meanings, convictions or traditions can be part of the context of a group or an individual. Hence, context(s) have an influence and define constraints for concrete practices and interactions, and the latter codetermine contexts as well.

Bibliography

Borofsky, Robert, Barth, Fredrik and Shweder, Richard, et al. 2001. 'WHEN: A Conversation about Culture', *American Anthropologist*, Vol. 103, No. 2: 432–46.

Bourdieu, Pierre. 1994. *La misère du monde*. Paris: Gallimard.

Cohen, Robert S. (ed.) 1964. *Selected Works of Otto Neurath*. New York: Reidel Publishers.

Evens Foundation. (ed.) 2002. *Europe's New Racism? Causes, Manifestations and Solutions*. New York: Berghahn Books.

Fabian, Johannes. 1984. *Time and the Other. How Anthropology Makes its Object*. New York: Columbia University Press.

Farella, John R. 1984. *The Main Stalk: A Synthesis of Navajo Philosophy*. Tucson: Arizona University Press.

Geertz, Clifford. 1973. *The Interpretation of Culture*. New York: Basic Books.

Hofstede, Geert. 1993. *Communication across Cultures*. London: Sage.

Huntington, Samuel P. 1996. *The Clash of Civilizations and the Remaking of the World Order*. New York: Simon and Schuster.

Kriesberg, Louis. 1994. *Conflict Resolution*. London: Lynne Riemer Publishers.

LeVine, Robert A. and Campbell, Donald T. 1972. *Ethnocentrism: Theories of Conflict, Ethnic Attitudes and Group Behavior*. New York: Wiley.

Lévi-Strauss, Claude. 1973. 'Race et histoire'. In *Anthropologie Structurale Deux*, ed. Claude Lévi-Strauss, 377–422. Paris: Plon.

Naroll, Raoul. 1983. *The Moral Order: An Introduction to the Human Situation*. London: Sage.

Pinxten, Rik. 1997. *When the Day Breaks: Essays in Anthropology and Philosophy*. Hamburg: P. Lang Verlag.

———— 1998. 'America for the Americans'. *In Distant Mirrors: America as a Foreign Culture*, eds. Philip R. Devita and James D. Amstrong, 100–108. Belmont, Cal.: Wadsworth.

———— and Farrer, Claire. 1993. 'A Comparative View of Learning'. In *Sociogenesis Reexamined*, eds. Willbrord De Graaf and Robert Maier, 169–84. New York: Springer.

———— and Verstraete, Ghislain (eds.) 1998. *Cultuur en macht* (Culture and Power). Antwerp: Hadewych.

Preston, P.W. 1998. *Political/Cultural Identity: Citizens and Nations in a Global Era*. London: Sage.

Roland, Alan. 1991. *In Search of the Self in India and Japan*. New York: SUNY Press.

Rubinstein, Robert. 2002. 'Anthropology, Peace and Human Rights. Social Justice and World Anthropology'. *Social Justice, Anthropology, Peace and Human Rights*, No. 3: 1–5.

Schnapper, Dominique. 1993. 'La Citoyenneté à l'Epreuve. Les Musulmans pendant la Guerre du Golf'. *Revue Française de Science Politique*, No. 43: 187–208.

Service, Elman R. 1989. *A Century of Controversy: Ethnological Issues from 1860 to 1960*. New York: Wiley.

Staal, Frits. 1988. *Rules Without Meaning: Rituals, Mantras and the Human Sciences*. Hamburg: P. Lang Verlag.

Turner, Victor. 1969. *The Ritual Process: Structure and Anti-Structure*. Chicago: Aldine Press.

Verstraete, Ghislain and Pinxten, Rik. 1998. 'Identiteit en conflict' (Identity and Conflict). In *Cultuur en macht* (Culture and Power), eds. Rik Pinxten and Ghislain Verstraete, 1–74. Antwerp: Hadewych.

———— Pyliser, Christoph, Cornelis, Marijke and Pinxten, Rik. 2000. *Onderzoek naar het profiel en de verwachtingen van enkele speciefieke doelgroepen van het onthaalbeleid in het kader van het Vlaams minderhedenbeleid, met name erkende vluchtelingen en ontvankelijk verklaarde asielzoekers enerzijds en volgmigranten andere dan Turken en Marokkanen anderzijds* (Research for the Flemish government on social migration and policy). Ghent: Gent University, CICI Reports.

1

RELIGION, SOCIETY AND IDENTITY: FROM CLAIMS TO SCIENTIFIC CATEGORIES?

Lieve Orye

Claiming Religion and Identity as Scientific Terms

In the Introduction to this book a new model for thinking about identity and culture is developed as an answer to earlier, problematic uses of these concepts in the human sciences as well as in politics. The term 'identity' is claimed as a scientific term and the model can simultaneously be seen as an instrument that allows us to take at least one step out of the limited culturalist and sociologist perspectives and as a means to direct research and build new theories. Many terms are currently being discussed and re-evaluated in the human sciences; 'identity', 'religion', 'culture', 'society' are but a few of them. In this article I will direct my attention to religious studies as a site, where one can witness intense discussion on the appropriateness of the term 'religion' as a scientific concept, as well as intense activity in developing alternative perspectives that go beyond the limited religion *sui generis* or religionist versus reductionist approaches. An analysis of these discussions and of the search for alternative kinds of religious studies is undertaken. The purpose is not so much to solve the problems within this discipline, as to see whether lessons can be drawn more generally for evaluating human scientific terms and for developing a perspective on 'us, human beings' outside such limited and limiting culturalist or religionist and sociologist approaches. Two authors will figure prominently in this exercise, their work and discussions being in part the data analysed, and in part – at least in the case of Cantwell Smith – the basis for a broader historical exercise and a possible starting point for a renewed thinking about 'us, human beings'.

Cantwell Smith's *The Meaning and End of Religion* (1962) can be considered a milestone in the self-reflexive turn in religious studies. As Luther Martin sees it, 'since at least the early 1960s, scholars of religion have been very aware that their "object" of study is a Western category' (Martin 2000: 95). In his book,

Cantwell Smith clearly demonstrates the need to study the history of 'religion' more thoroughly, in order to lay bare its underlying presuppositions that may be responsible for a limitation of the questions asked and the answers sought for. More recently, further exercises in this self-reflection have brought authors like Russell McCutcheon (1997) and Kenneth Surin (1990a, 1990b) to point out that religious studies have been held captive in a discourse with a strong ideological, that is, liberal theological character. A liberal theological inheritance had directed most of the attention to issues of religious pluralism and the possibility of a peaceful coexistence of religions. For Cantwell Smith, and for the second scholar put upon the stage here, Ninian Smart, this issue of religious diversity and intolerance informed their lifelong projects of developing a new framework for religious studies. Both tried to bypass the older idea of religion as a separate sphere, reconceptualised the problems within the field and searched for new answers. However, McCutcheon's and Surin's verdict is a tough one when applied to Smith's and Smart's oeuvre. Presented as the result of scientific work, the latter's proposals for one or another kind of religious pluralism, or similar projects of global theology (Smith) or 'federations of the mind' (Smart), can be shown to be forms of imperialism in the very friendly disguise of tolerance. In other words, intolerance or ethnocentrism has not been left behind. Rather, it was 'dressed up', disguised and presented as tolerance and dialogue between equals.

On the one hand, contrasting Smith's and Smart's work and ideas about religious diversity, religion, identity and conflict will lead to both a confirmation and refinement of McCutcheon's and Surin's statements. For this exercise, the identity model as proposed in the Introduction, will appear as a useful instrument to show the limits of this hegemonic discourse that hampers religious studies in their academic pursuits. On the other hand, in this exercise I will simultaneously show that the accusation of disguised imperialism cannot imply that the work of any author tainted by it is simply to be relegated to the dustbin without further evaluation. In particular, I will show that some of Cantwell Smith's doubts could contain the beginnings of a healthy exercise in thinking about religion and identity and about 'us, human beings' more generally.

The main focus of this book is not religious studies, nor the particular problems within this field of study. However, by focusing on scholars of religion, I hope to show that when the concern is the extraction of terms from hegemonic discourses in view of their reclamation as scientific terms, a study of their history is a highly useful exercise. Moreover, in taking Smith's historical exercise a few steps further, giving attention to 'religion' as a political term and as related to the invention of 'society', one finds the histories of religion and identity entangled. Finally, from this more comprehensive history one can derive lessons to be learned for religious studies and human sciences more generally. It makes clear that the problem of liberal theological colouring, still present in the writings of Smith and Smart, should be viewed as part of a larger issue that once fostered but now hampers the development of the human sciences.

In a first step, I will introduce and contrast the two protagonists, Cantwell Smith and Ninian Smart. In a next step, Smith's historical exercise will be out-

lined and elaborated on in such a way that an entangled history of 'religion' and
'identity' appears. In a further step, it will become clear that although changes
in society are not a mere result of changing ideas, a particular impact of ideas,
theories and the human sciences is unmistakable. The latter fact cannot be
ignored in evaluating concepts and theories about religion and identity. However, I agree with many religious studies scholars that, notwithstanding his
valuable historical study of the terms 'religion' and 'belief', Smith did conclude
too quickly that the concept of 'religion' was to be thrown overboard, implying
parallel conclusions for 'identity'. These conclusions need reconsidering, especially because it will become clear that Smith's hastiness to end his historical
study in view of formulating an alternative perspective was informed by an
extra-scientific motive. Furthermore, I share the opinion that his perspective in
terms of 'faith' and 'cumulative tradition' has strong religious overtones which
are inappropriate for science. However, by once again contrasting his work
with that of Ninian Smart, I will argue that if one is willing to read between his
– steeped in religious language – lines, it contains hypotheses that are well
worth considering in a study of religion and identity outside the modern liberal
framework.

Contrasting Cantwell Smith and Ninian Smart

Cantwell Smith and Ninian Smart, who both have to a great extent determined
the landscape in religious studies since the 1960s and 1970s, argued for fundamental change in the discipline and put a lot of effort into developing a new
programme for it. Both argued strongly against a mere reduction of the subject
matter as they saw envisaged in the social sciences, and also pleaded against the
irrationalisation and subsequent safeguarding of some 'religious essence'. Religious diversity was a central focus for these authors and they both fought
against the essentialisation of religious traditions. However, this latter cause
both authors pursued in a very different way. The difference can be seen as follows: Ninian Smart does not shy away from using the word 'identity', whereas
Cantwell Smith strongly felt that question marks were in order here.

In Smart's view, religious traditions give the material to construct an identity.
Such tradition provides the participant with a world view, a meaningful picture
of the universe, and of one's place in this universe. It pictures possible goals in
life, gives moral prescriptions, and so on. Smart is thrilled by the new developments in which people become conscious of their own religious tradition as different from others and embark on a search for what is distinctive, what is
unique in theirs. He speaks about a phase of solidification of traditions because
they found themselves in contrast with one another and became self-conscious
about their identity (Smart 1992: 23). We are moving into 'a new world era', he
says, in which a dialogue between self-conscious traditions will lead to a growing tolerance and learning from each other through 'mutually friendly criticism'. At the same time he is aware that things can go, and are often going, in
quite a different direction, turning out far more violently than 'friendly criti-

cism'. However, a solution is suggested within his new programme for religious studies that is nonreductive, nonessentialist and based on a 'soft epistemology'. For Smart it is clear that once one starts looking at world-views and religious traditions as complex, dynamic, organic collages with several dimensions, situated in social, cultural, political, historical contexts, one can only apply a soft epistemology which allows for statements about the truth between world-views rather than about the truth of a world-view in itself. Such soft epistemology implies the necessity of a 'sensitive' epistemology; in other words, it rejects clinging to an exclusivism in which one considers one's own tradition as true, while condemning the others, which are seen as false. As far as Ninian Smart is concerned, the recent transformations can go two ways. Either his programme of 'mutually friendly criticism' based on a soft epistemology is accepted and a glorious period will arrive, or traditions as well as nonreligious world-views will cling to an unarguable exclusivism, with conflict and war being the inevitable result. The idea that a dialogue between religions, especially world religions, is necessary and will turn the world into a better place in which to live is widespread in religious studies, as is the idea that religious studies themselves should contribute to this scenario. Similar ideas can be found in Cantwell Smith's proposal for religious studies and for a global theology. However, interesting differences can be found between him and Ninian Smart.

Ninian Smart takes a solidification of traditions for granted, as an almost natural development given the process of globalisation, and sees the grounds for conflict mainly in different truth-claims and practice-claims. He seeks a solution for possible conflict within this constellation, by softening the sharp edges of arguments about and judgements of these claims. Cantwell Smith, however, albeit similarly delighted about the possibilities that are opening up in our days, strongly problematises the recent trend towards reification and talk in terms of 'beliefs', 'propositional truth', 'a religion', 'identity' and argues against it. Contrary to Smart, Smith is not so eager to use the word 'identity'. He writes (Smith and Burbridge 1997: 96):

> It sometimes goes unnoticed in the West, that most Westerners long since traded in their soul for a self, a considerably more individualist and mundane, indeed isolated and self-centered, concept; and in recent decades even that seems to be giving way to an identity, rather – except that no one seems to have an identity: it would appear to be something that we are all supposedly in search of.

Underlying these differences, a different theoretical project can be found. Smith is cautious about some recent developments in Western society and throughout the world in general that lead to a reification of very dynamic and constantly changing religious traditions into 'a religion'. The latter can be described as a politics of religion, more recently evolving into a politics of identity that involves not only scholars and officials but also the believers themselves in what Smith characterises as primarily a *secular* process. As Don Wiebe (1991: 131) indicates:

Smith was not concerned that this process of reification created (presumed the existence of) some metaphysical reality that was to be found embodied in particular cultural configurations but rather that particular cultural configurations were being taken to possess a distinguishable unity, coherence and identity in themselves, quite independently of any relationship to such a transcendent reality. This, according to Smith, was to intellectualize the concept of religion and to miss the essential meaning of the term that its history reveals – its disclosure of a supernatural reality that lies beyond the social, historical and ideological components of human existence. ... The only proper understanding of 'religion' for Smith, therefore, is one that will allow the world 'to respond to a transcendent and concerned reality'.

The transcendent as a hypothesis or principle is crucial to Smith. It is an element in his work that is often misunderstood as the introduction of an a priori theological proposition. However, the latter goes totally against the spirit of his work. As will become clear further on, Smith saw its introduction as the only way to take up a position outside the framework he criticised so thoroughly. The main problem for him is not, as Ninian Smart argues, that several dimensions are left out of the picture, or that the organic and dynamic character of religious traditions is lost out of sight. He sees the error in the depersonalisation and detranscendentalisation implied in this trend of reification and solidification, mainly because it leads to an impoverished and intellectualised image of us, human beings. Similarly, the idea that theologians should nurture 'the Christian identity' must have seemed as strange to him as the idea of believing in a certain religion. Both ideas are of recent origin. As Smith pointed out, one used to nurture one's or another's relation to God and one used to believe in God. However, a series of transformations during the Renaissance, the Enlightenment and later, in which 'religion' received its modern content, redirected attention from a personal relationship with a transcendent reality to the this-worldly observable tradition, putting the main light on impersonal beliefs and propositions. Smith deplored these changes and argued these had disastrous consequences for people's religious life. He concluded that the scientific use of terms connected to these transformations could only lead to misapprehension and distortion and to a further weakening of religious life. As an alternative to 'religion' he suggested the combination of 'faith' and 'cumulative tradition'. The exchange would improve religious studies and, so Smith hoped, would allow for a highly necessary religious revival within our modern Western society.

Religious overtones must make us hesitant in endorsing Smith's views and hopes. However, carrying further his historical exercise will make clear why Smith relies on religious language and will give an opportunity to extract some interesting hypotheses from under this religious dust. Two elements will be important in the following historical narrative. Firstly, religion is not only a secular, but also a thoroughly political term. Secondly, the shift towards politics will draw our attention to the role of the intellectual in the coming about of our modern Western society.

Outline of an Entangled History of Religion and Identity

'Religion' as a Secular or Outsider's Term

Cantwell Smith is known for his historical study of terms such as 'religion' and 'belief'. Both terms have undergone drastic changes since the Middle Ages. His early work in 1962 was later supplemented by that of other scholars, focusing mainly on 'religion' as the descriptive term for the subject matter of religious studies. All scholars seem to agree that the Renaissance and Enlightenment period brought radical changes that inform our use of the concepts 'religion' and 'belief'. Next to the discovery of other continents and people with different rituals and beliefs, the crisis of authority and the religious wars played an important role. There is a difference of opinion whether these wars were the result of earlier important changes and merely gave these processes of transformation a further impetus or twist, or whether they can be regarded as a primary cause, urging theologians, philosophers and politicians to search for radically new solutions and forging the opening up of what once seemed a stable worldview and social organisation. Most scholars nevertheless agree that 'religion' is a *secular* term, as Cantwell Smith has it. However, in order to steer away from the religious overtones attached to this characterisation, one might prefer Jonathan Z. Smith's[1] (1982) terminology here. He sees the modern term 'religion' as an outsider or 'second order term', invented and dependent for its existence on the study of religion. According to J.Z. Smith, the term can only be used to characterise others from a distant position. Cantwell Smith would agree with such a characterisation, as Idinopulos confirms: 'The word, religion, comes into usage not as the participant's word but as the observer's word, one that focuses on observable doctrines, institutions, ceremonies, and other practices. By contrast, faith is about the nonobservable, life-shaping vision of transcendence held by a participant' (Idinopulos 1998: 77).

In *Imagining Religion* Jonathan Z. Smith (1982) points out that people have had their entire history to be religious, but that only Western man has had the last few centuries to imagine religion. Similarly, a pluralism of religious traditions was not an entirely new thing belonging to our recent history. However, the objectification of 'the other' as a source of systematic knowledge 'about', was. In other words, only recently was 'religion' imagined as a subject matter to be studied from an outsider position, a position originally taken by Christian theologians in an attempt to answer the questions that the existence of people with other strange rituals and religious practices evoked. Gradually, but in the end decisively, there was no room in this exercise for any transcendence or god, and initiative shifted from theologians to philosophers and scientists. In a way, this shift coincided with a change in attention from ritual to virtue and later on to beliefs as the defining characteristic of religion. In their turn, these transformations mentioned by Jonathan Z. Smith are part of what can be seen as the outcome of the crisis of authority within Christianity.

Whereas Aquinas had tried to solve the question of multiple authorities by introducing a hierarchy giving the Bible the highest authority, followed by the Church Fathers and so on, Luther argued against hierarchy and introduced his *sola scriptura* rule. However, this rule was not without problems of interpretation. On the one hand, it resulted in an emphasis on absolute certainty, and on the other, in privileging inner conviction and individual conscience. As a consequence, faith was safeguarded from debate while at the same time the number of authorities multiplied indefinitely. Scepticism radicalised and internal discord within Christianity increased dramatically. As Jeffrey Stout (1981) points out in *The Flight from Authority*, Descartes took part in this struggle and gave a historically specific answer in which philosophy and science became the means to settle the debate. His answer, which incorporated the element of inner certainty and put aside tradition and authority, consisted of the rehabilitation of the category of scientia, by taking geometry and arithmetic as examples of absolute certain knowledge, built up from self-evident basic propositions. Stout considers Descartes' answer historically specific, although it has informed philosophy ever since. Only a decade after Descartes' death, an alternative solution was given in the formulation of the New Probability, which was based on a tempered scepticism and the idea that degrees of probability could be calculated without the need to appeal to authority. It was this solution that was to pervade society and science. However, in both cases the result is similar. Tradition is disqualified, the focus is on beliefs as propositions, and the relationship between faith and reason is reversed.

In the subsequent discussions between philosophers and theologians the transition provoked a change of mysteries into uncomfortable paradoxes with very low probability, a shift which had problematic consequences for the Christian faith. The latter found itself in a defensive position within a discourse in which it no longer determined the rules. Alasdair MacIntyre (1969: 25–26) describes its dilemma as follows:

> [A]ny presentation of theism which is able to secure a hearing from a secular audience has undergone a transformation that has evacuated it entirely of its theistic content. Conversely, any presentation which retains such theistic content will be unable to secure the place in contemporary culture which those theologians desire for it.

Cantwell Smith deplores these developments. Their equivalent in the study of religion results in a distortion. The subject matter is detranscendentalised and intellectualised by taking the observable externalia and 'beliefs', such as 'the belief that God exists' or 'the belief that there is a transcendent reality', as their central elements. In such a distorted view, MacIntyre's dilemma is merely a logical outcome. But Smith has more reasons to lament these developments. This detranscendentalisation and intellectualisation had broader social ramifications. They gradually came to pervade almost all aspects of our life, changing 'a living in truth' into 'a living according to truths which have a propositional character'. For religious people, 'I believe', meaning '[g]iven the reality of God, as a fact of the universe, I hereby proclaim that I align my life accordingly, pledging love and loyalty', changed into 'I believe' as '[g]iven the uncertainty of God, as a fact of modern life, so-and-so reports that the idea of God is part of the furniture of his mind' (Smith 1979: 118). The first statement is a statement about the kind of relationship one wants to have with another being, in this case God. The second statement is entirely a statement about oneself and one's inner space. It consists of a self-reflection in which the content of one's mind is the subject matter. Smith's allergy for terms such as 'self' and 'identity' has to do with his disapproval of the latter scenario that he considers entirely secular. The use of these terms as well as of the term 'religion', by the faithful themselves, lures them into a secular rather than religious activity, directing the attention to observable, this-worldly things and to themselves as individuals who some-where in their heads hold a belief, possibly a doubt, that God exists. In what fol-lows, I want to add an interesting extra dimension to Smith's history. Attila Molnar (2002) has pointed to the political character of the term 'religion'. His historical narrative makes clear that religion as an outsider term was conceptu-alised from a specific point of view with certain political goals in mind.

Religion as a Political Term

Attila Molnar (2002) has recently argued that 'religion' as we use the word today emerged as a foster child of the religious wars during the Reformation, a period in which many of our basic notions, such as 'politics' and the modern notion of 'state', were constructed. His central thesis is that 'religion' was constructed from a political point of view by lay 'politicians' and by political theology, as a scepti-cal translation of the Christian notions of *conscientia* and *universitas fidelium*.[2] The Christian tradition considered man sinful and therefore in need of control, both from within by God and from without by worldly power. The idea was that both were necessary and that these were indispensable for a society to endure, an idea shared by church and worldly powers. As a consequence, those who did not believe in another reality and in the possibility of punishment for one's sins after this life were seen as potential rebels and disturbers of the peace. However, the Reformation brought some fundamental changes in the notion of conscien-tia. Martin Luther developed a highly individualised and emotionalised inter-pretation of the notion that had previously meant 'knowledge shared with others'. These changes not only created problems within the Christian world, but for the worldly powers as well. Luther considered conscientia the ultimate judge above the rule of worldly power because it was seen as resulting from a direct relation between the faithful person and God. For him, conscientia was always good, infallible and homogeneous among faithful Christians. Because the true Christian was directed by God, there was no need for laws or government. The ultimate authority was interiorised, individual and nonrational; the original intersubjective character was lost. As an attempted solution to the crisis of authority it only led to its intensification.

The religious wars, resulting from this crisis, and the discovery of a vast reli-gious world outside of Christianity had urged political thinkers, such as diplo-mats Jean Bodin and Herbert of Cherbury, to answer the question of religious truth by independent criteria. In other words, they took a position outside the religious traditions and tried to find an answer without invoking God or any other transcendent being, hoping that this would bring a solution to the con-flicts. In *Explaining Religion*, Samuel Preus (1987) devotes his first two chapters to these diplomats, arguing that the seeds for a naturalistic discourse on religion are to be found in their work. Bodin was the first to objectify religion by transcending the accepted and contradictory confessional frameworks available to him. 'He brought religion itself into intellectual focus as a problem (the problem of contradictory absolute claims without criteria for solution) which could only be approached fruitfully from a perspective that would transcend contemporary confessional norms' (Preus 1987: xiv). He became convinced that the uncovering of the first origin of religion would be the key to making possible a rational judgement about religion.

However, the problem of authority, culminating in its intensification through Luther's individualisation and emotionalisation, gave political thinkers a new problem to address: how to argue for a political society? It is in answering this question that 'religion' received its secular interpretation. As Molnar points out, religion took the role of *conscientia*, but the link with the transcendent was erased. The notion of 'religion' had a sceptical meaning and was significantly indifferent to doctrinal differences and to arguments about doctrinal truth. In other words, as with Bodin and Herbert of Cherbury, 'religion' as a political notion was an outsider term. In their reflection on political society, political theologians and lay thinkers transformed Cicero's term 'religio' into 'religion' as referring to shared common moral rules. Religion was seen as a necessary control from within. It complemented and supported the necessary control from without by worldly government. It referred to a shared, intersubjective knowledge, not in the form of dogmas, which had unwanted social-political consequences, but in the form of immanent moral rules with this-worldly consequences. Opposed to the Christian *conscientia*, religion did not provide the political community with a substantive *universitas fidelium*, but with a formal one. Most important was not that the faithful thought the same things, but that they thought in the same way, 'religiously'. Religion in the latter sense entailed obedience to the laws of nature and the bounds of duty. The purpose was no longer to discuss divine matters in order to find a solution, but tolerance, this-worldly political peace and a way of living together without the need of doctrinal unity. A separation between church and state, between religion and politics lay ahead. The formal concept of religion as a shared inner control common to the differing sects and faiths, made it possible for Bodin to argue that the state could and should be indifferent to the affairs of divinity, without undermining its possibility. In the end, the problem of religious truth was not solved, but circumvented. In this constellation, it was important to be religious and much better to have a false religion than no religion at all.

Religion and Society

The sceptical idea of 'religion' has been very important in subsequent political thought. We can see it plays a crucial role in what Eric Wolf (1988: 754) has called the 'invention of Society' as 'different from the state, a separate and distinctive entity, as the arena of interplay of private rights against the state'. John Locke's political and theological ideas, contrasted to those of Thomas Hobbes, are extremely interesting in this respect.

Thomas Hobbes was one of the first who set out to identify the *secular* sources of political power that could provide for security and stability. His insight that political order can emerge as a result of human rather than divine efforts is seen as heralding modern political thought (Reynolds and Saxonhouse 1995: 124). Rather than pointing out foundations in religion, Hobbes saw a solution for civil disorders in a sovereign authority backed with force. However, he was aware that force was insufficient unless people were educated in obedience. According to Hobbes, religious and civil wars were caused by those doctrines and ideas taught in universities and preached from the pulpit that encouraged people into disobedience. As Geraint Parry (1998: 13) points out, Hobbes had a highly intellectualist view of the nature of social conflict. Knowledge is power. Language is seen as the prime means of division, because it can be used to advance individual interests. However, Hobbes held the opinion that division could be avoided if there were only one kind of knowledge and one power. What he had in mind was the civil power in the hands of the sovereign as the representative of the multitude. 'No interpretation should be allowed to appeal to a higher authority than the civil one. Especially dangerous is the belief in immaterial bodies like spirits, ghosts or souls, that people can wave around in order to transcend the force, the flesh and the authority of civil power' (Latour 1990: 150). Consequently, in Hobbes's view, religion and morality are dependent on the sovereign. It is he who holds the last word about what is right and wrong and about matters of faith. Put differently, there is neither morality nor religion before the founding of the state. 'For where Laws be wanting, there neither Religion, nor Life, nor society can be maintained' (Hobbes in Reynolds and Saxonhouse 1995: 149). As Parry (1998: 719) notes, for Hobbes, faith is 'not acquired by inspiration but is learned by education and discipline which it was the responsibility of the sovereign to provide'. For Hobbes, then, civil society is not separate from the state; the possibility of the interplay of private rights against the state is out of the question. The sceptical idea of religion as commonly shared values is already present here; however, it is seen as a matter completely in the hands of the sovereign.

Quite different ideas can be found in John Locke's work. Arguing against the idea that the structure of government derived from the paternal powers of the first human father,[3] with descent justifying absolute monarchy, Locke asserted that government was limited. Contrary to Hobbes, Locke believed that men's original state of nature was 'a state of perfect freedom to order their actions, and dispose of their possessions and persons as they think fit, within the bounds of the law of Nature, without asking leave or depending upon the will of any other man. A state also of equality, wherein all the power and jurisdiction is reciprocal...' (Locke 1690: §2.4). This state of Nature was governed by the law of Nature which could be known by reason and which taught that 'being all equal and independent, no one ought to harm another in his life, health, liberty or possessions' (ibid. §2.6). However, because in the state of nature each was one's own judge and because there was no protection against those who lived outside the law of nature, a state was formed by social contract. For Locke, 'civil government is the proper remedy for the inconveniences of the state of Nature' (ibid. §2.13). However, it could only exist by virtue of the consent of the governed. 'I, moreover, affirm that all men are naturally in that state, and remain so till, by their own consents, they make themselves members of some politic society' (ibid. §2.15). And when people 'are united into one body and have a common established law and judicature to appeal to, with authority to decide controversies between them and punish offenders... [they] are in civil society with one another' (ibid. §7.87). This civil society was and had to be essentially different from natural society. It had to support and to perfect the latter by adding a *juridical* dimension that could secure the reasonableness of society (Goyard-Fabre 1988: 202–203). Contrary to Hobbes then, Locke does not see the state of nature as denied by the institution of civil government. Rather, by installing a common law and judicature it remedies its shortcomings and contrarieties. At the same time, for Locke this essential juridical dimension was also the reason why civil society did not merely coincide with the state or government. Dissolution of the latter did not imply a dissolution of the former:

> What reappears when the government is dissolved, is a sovereign body animated by a unique will and authorized to interpret the law of nature, not a collection of individuals each with their own conscience ... society ... can subsist, with its relations of juridical obligation that connect the individuals towards the decisions of the majority, once the government is disappeared. (Spitz 1993: 62–63)[4]

Here, society appears as 'different from the state, a separate and distinctive entity' (Wolf 1988: 754).

However, Locke's concept of 'society' contains a dilemma. 'Men are set free to pursue their own interests, as abstract individuals; but there is really no guarantee other than pious hope that they will be able to adjudicate conflicts among themselves' (Wolf 1988: 754). Locke looks for a solution to this problem in God. He sees the latter as governing not as an omnipotent patriarch, but through morality enshrined in the heart of each of us. As Louis Dumont puts it, 'for Locke to conceive a society as the juxtaposition of abstract individuals was possible only because for the concrete bonds of society he could substitute morality... because Christianity warranted the individual as a moral being' (Dumont in Wolf 1988: 754). It will soon become clear that this moral being is in fact rather a juridical being capable of taking responsibility. As Simone Goyard-Fabre (1988: 212–13) sees it, Locke did not, contrary to Hobbes, evict God out of the political sphere. Rather, based on the ontologies and teleologies of the Creation, he makes men responsible for how things are going. Thanks to God, people in civil society are no longer individuals but persons (ibid. 203). In other words, the Christian God appears in his views as a kind of superego or inner spectator, as the glue that holds society together (Wolf 1988: 754). Nevertheless, though Locke refers to the Christian God, he in fact uses the word 'religion' with a doctrinally indifferent meaning. This becomes even clearer when in his essays on toleration he argues for broad religious freedom while at the same time making an exception for atheism and Roman Catholicism because he thought these to be inimical to religion and the state.

In its turn the idea of society as a reality in itself would subsequently, in conjunction with a growing intellectualisation, inform the further history of the notion of religion. Cantwell Smith confirmed that the notion of religion as a particular system of belief embodied in a bounded community was unknown prior to the modern period. It was, as John Hick phrased it,

> after the red-hot volcanic experience and thought of the great reformers had cooled into the abstract disputes of the seventeenth century, that the notion of a religion as a system of doctrines was effectively formed. There was soon joined to this the thought of the human population which professes and preserves these doctrines, so that by the eighteenth century the understanding of 'religions' as alternative systems of belief embodied in mutually exclusive ideological communities had become accepted. The nineteenth century added the historical dimension, perceiving the phenomena now called Islam, Hinduism, Christianity, Buddhism, etc. as *complex organisms*, each with its own long history, which nineteenth and twentieth century scholarship has traced [some would say 'invented'] and studied in increasing particularity. (Hick in Smith 1962: xii, italics and insertion added)

What is important in this historical narrative on the invention of 'society', says Eric Wolf (1988: 755), is that 'from the beginning that concept of freely interacting individuals also carried with it a warrant of common values. Ever since then Society, a society, has been seen as the repository of common values'. In other words, religion as a secularised version of the Christian notions of conscientia and universitas fidelium has become part of a central modern notion. God, however, died, 'we killed him', said Nietzsche, but according to Wolf, his legacy was taken over by the Nation that turned Society into a project. With the Christian and religious traditions being more and more in a defensive position, other terms took over the meaning of the sceptical term religion. Culture, ideology, etc. come to mind. These terms, as well as the presumptions on which they rest, have invaded not only political thought, but the human sciences as well.

Christine Helliwell and Barry Hindess (1999) have pointed out two presumptions that are pervasive in the human sciences. The presumption of ideational unity refers to the idea that large-scale social unities are to be understood as defined or held together by *shared values, concepts or understandings*. The presumption of systemic unity involves the idea that these unities also have to be understood as *self-regulating, boundary-maintaining social systems*. 'Societies', 'cultures', 'religions' are most of the time understood in these terms. The idea behind these concepts is that such an ideational unity serves to structure human thought and behaviour and as such orders sociality. 'Religion' as a sceptical political term seems to be at the basis of the first presumption, and, as the historical narrative seems to imply, it has opened the door to the second one.[5] A third presumption should also be given attention. The idea of society as separate from and more sturdy and robust than nature was present in Hobbes's invention of the naked calculating citizen whose competence it is to hold property and to be represented through the artificial construction of the Sovereign (Latour 1990: 158–59). The latter idea of abstract individuals joined by a human, artificial construction, a social contract, was taken over by John Locke. Together with the third presumption that places nature versus society, it has been a core element in the human sciences ever since.

'Identity' Involved

The concept of 'identity' forms part of the historical narrative outlined here. Yves Charles Zarka (1993) argues that Locke took up Hobbes's theory of identity and developed it further. This resulted in an important transition, going from a Hobbesian way of thinking about identity without 'ipseity' to the emergence of the latter in Lockian thinking. Hobbes, as well as Locke, developed a theory of identity as a way to substitute the insolvable metaphysical problem of individuation by a search for types of identity in relation to the way we perceive and name things. The question is no longer whether identity is a question of matter or form, or the aggregate of all coincidences. Different types exist. Hobbes can argue that the identity of a man or city or an animal is not the same as the identity of a body. In the first cases there is identity because the actions and thoughts derive from the same principle that guides their generation, whereas the latter is an identity because the size rests the same. A man once born is still the same in his old age, although his body may have changed thoroughly. Locke continues this line of thought in which different irreducible types of identity can be discerned, but he goes beyond it by also theorising about a personal identity. Hobbes does not pose this question of self-identity, reducing the identity of man to a mere identity of form. Furthermore, he thinks about 'identity', 'consciousness' and 'person' as three separate issues, whereas Locke will combine these three to arrive at something quite different: the emergence of 'ipseity'.

However, Locke's intention behind his theory of identity is very different from Hobbes's: he wants to determine the concept of the person who recognises his thoughts and actions as his own, so that these can be seen as proper to him and for which he can be held responsible. In other words, says Zarka, Locke's intention is essentially moral in nature. His 'personal identity' gives a definite foundation for morality and turns people into juridical persons fit to live in civil society (Zarka 1993: 18, 19). For Locke the moral person and the juridical person are closely linked and both make a society possible. '[I]n this *personal identity* is founded all Right and Justice of Reward and Punishment' (Locke in Zarka 1993: 19). The common morality needed as glue between abstract individuals to form a society is possible, according to Locke, because we are each 'a thinking intelligent being' capable to consider our selves as our selves, as the same in different times and places, and to see our actions and thoughts as our own and take responsibility for them. The latter form of identity thus differs fundamentally from other forms (substance and form), since it is no longer based on the permanence of something objective or objectifiable, but on an interior apprehension of oneself which extends from the present into the past.

With this original contribution to political thought, Locke participates in what Zarka (1999) calls 'the invention of the subject of the law', a central figure in modernity. Contrary to the 'identity of man' as an example of the identity of form, the personal identity marks a difference between human beings and animals and implies a definition of man as a being to whom rights are related naturally, simply because he is human (Zarka 1999: 245). Locke's theory on personal identity shows the opening up of a new discursive space. The latter is linked to a specific epistemic structure in which subjective consciousness filled with private beliefs and objective facts are seen as two separate domains, to be dealt with in the first case by religion, in the second by politics. Within this space, new questions *of* authenticity, sincerity,[6] agency, and responsibility could be posed, as well as new questions *about* human beings, society and religion. The newly invented inner space could be explored and developed and a politics of personal identity and of consciousness – according to Talal Asad (1996: 265) an entirely modern Western possibility – could develop.

Second-order Concepts as Claims

Smith's Misgivings

Cantwell Smith's historical study of the terms 'religion' and 'belief' made him highly critical about their usefulness. He sees these terms as secular, objective, outsider terms that direct attention to what is observable, or objectifiable. Significant, however, is that in evaluating them, he does not limit himself to scientific arguments. Oxtoby summarises Smith's position as follows:

> Objectivity is objectionable in a twofold sense: when people are treated as objects, not only human community is threatened, but proper intellectual understanding. Such interpretations, however factually correct they may seem, should be *abandoned as morally wrong because they disrupt community*; but moreover, they are for Smith conceptually wrong because they fail to take adequate account of persons. (Smith and Oxtoby 1982: 159, italics inserted)

Whereas Oxtoby seems to take the moral sense for granted and presents Smith's scientific concerns as the more astonishing element, I see both as significant. Scientifically speaking, Cantwell Smith's problem with the secularity of the term 'religion' is, apart from the religious overtones, similar to what Pierre Bourdieu called the scholastic error. Smith writes in a similar vein about the fallacy of misplaced logic. The latter is committed whenever the question of propositional truth is asked about a personal religious reality. One uses logic to answer a wrongly posed question about a subject matter that in the event is misunderstood. The truth of religious traditions is not so much a matter of logical or propositional truth as it is a matter of evaluating the possibilities and transformations these traditions bring about in people's lives.

Morally speaking, Smith points to a further reason why he rejects the term 'religion'. The secular term 'religion', denoting from an outsider position the activities one as a human being can be involved in oneself, as well as the specific intellectualistic form of agency and self-reflexivity connected with it, has seeped through in ways of being religious, thus contributing to a further secularisation of Western society. The issue here is what some would call the 'spillover effect' or 'reflexivity' of human science that is in contrast with natural science of a rather particular type. Bugs and maize do not change because science has opened up a new conceptual space that somehow becomes available to them, leading to new ways of behaving and new ways of leading a life, yet people do. For Cantwell Smith these spill-over effects have not resulted in a success story. This seeping through resulted in a fundamental change with quite detrimental effects. The peculiarity of the change is clear in Ernest Gellner's similar remark about the term 'culture':

> The modern nationalist consciously wills his identification with a culture. His overt consciousness of his own culture is already, in historical perspective, an interesting oddity. Traditional man revered his city or clan through its deity or shrine, using the one, as Durkheim insisted so much, as a token for the other. He lacked any concept of 'culture'... He knew the gods of this culture, but not the culture itself. In the age of nationalism, all this is changed twice over; the shared culture is revered directly and not through the haze of some token, and the entity so revered is diffuse, internally undifferentiated, and insists that a veil of forgetfulness should discreetly cover obscure internal differences. (Gellner 1987: 10)

Cantwell Smith gave a lot of attention to the effects of this transition, uttering his misgivings about them, but left the study of how it came about mostly to others. His contribution is limited to pointing out a certain omnivorous dialectic that installs itself once one party uses the discourse in terms of beliefs and externals as the discourse for contestation. I quote Smith at length here because his own account is so compact and telling.

> The intellectualisation of the concept of 'religion' was part of the emerging claim of the mind to understand the universe and assert its domination; but it is part, also, of a response to the strident claims of many religious groups to refute each other. When one is setting forth one's own faith, one speaks of something deep, personal, and transcendentally oriented. If one uses the term 'religion' then, this is what one spontaneously means. If, on the other hand, one is rejecting what other people set forth – in and through which one does not oneself find or see any transcendent orientation, at least no valid one – then one necessarily conceptualises it in terms of its outward manifestations, since these are all that is available. One's own 'religion' may be piety and faith, obedience, worship, and a vision of God. An alien 'religion' is a system of beliefs or rituals, an abstract and impersonal pattern of observables. A dialectic ensues, however. If one's own 'religion' is attacked, by unbelievers who conceptualise it schematically, or all religion is, by the indifferent, one tends to leap to the defence of what is attacked, so that presently participants of a faith – especially those most involved in the argument – are using the term in the same externalist and theoretical sense as are their opponents. (Smith 1962: 42–43)

Smith sees two developments arising from this. One is the use of the plural 'religions'. The second is the concept of a generic 'religion' to designate as an external entity the total system or sum of all systems of beliefs, or simply the generalisation that they are there. He seems to hint at the political character of the latter when he states that the concept was primarily formulated and used by men who were weary of the clash between religious groups or suspicious of the whole religious enterprise (ibid. 43). For Smith, both the plural and the generic term are intrinsically linked with contemplation from the outside. These arise, he says, when one abstracts, depersonalises, and reifies the various systems of other people of which one does not oneself see the meaning or appreciate the point, let alone accept the validity. Smith makes clear that once one party in the dialogue resorts to a discourse in terms of beliefs, the other is silenced, irrationalised or forced to argue within its limits. Ironically then, if we take the connection between religion as a sceptical notion and the notions of society and identity seriously, it appears that this sceptical notion contributed to the installation of a hegemonic discourse in which a religious dimension was looked at, studied about and judged and defended within a particular intellectualistic perspective, resulting in a segregation and intellectualisation of what once, according to Smith, belonged to the very centre of life.

However, giving attention to the other terms in our entangled history leads to a much more encompassing perspective in which the dialectic is not limited to the religious dimension, as Gellner's statement about 'culture' has already made clear. The narrative of this peculiar transformation can be told in much more detail. Briefly, it refers to a process in which outsider concepts as claims made from a peculiar 'free-floating' position, and containing strong traces of this position, were made into *a* reality through theory and practice.[7] Let me give a small outline.

Concepts as Intellectuals' Claims? The Coproduction of Science, Intellectuals and Their Social Context

In *Leviathan and the Air-pump: Hobbes, Boyle and the Experimental Life* (1985) Steven Shapin and Simon Schaffer argued that the idea of politics and science as separate found its origin in boundary-speech and the development of boundary-conventions. Bruno Latour denotes the subject matter of this book as the *co-production* of science and its social context. Both Boyle and Hobbes struggled to invent a science *and* a context *and* a divide between the two. Both were concerned about putting an end to religious and civil wars, and both saw the problem as a matter of authority. Latour (1990: 159) summarises their importance and influence as follows:

> They are two Founding Fathers, drafting *one* and the same constitution but writing in their draft that their Branches should have *no* relation whatsoever. They conspire to make one and the same innovation in political theory: to science the representation of non-humans and no possibility of influence by or appeal to politics; to politics the representation of citizens with no influence by or relation to the non-humans produced and mobilized by science and technology.

However, though the original boundary-speech between natural science and politics has been firmly in place ever since, Locke's alternative ideas of civil society as a reality in itself, which could be seen as separate from government, opened up a new space in which intellectuals could think about the naked calculating citizen and society without interference and separate from state power (Bauman 1987). That is, the unity of authority was sliced up once more, granting philosophers and human scientists 'freedom of thought' and a space of their own in which consensus was the new, revolutionary criterion of truth. Where Hobbes had already turned (or invented) the social world as malleable by human sovereign hands, Locke changed it into a world in which, on the one hand, there was room for a self-regulating individual, while on the other hand, the philosopher-human scientist could find as subject matter a social reality of self-regulating processes of interaction.[8]

The second slicing up of authority, however, came with seeds for a new political reality demanding a new kind of knowledge and a new role for the intellectual. Hobbes and Locke contributed with their ideas to the establishment in the seventeenth and eighteenth centuries of what Helliwell and Hindess (1999) call 'the figure of the population of the state' as an object of knowledge and of governmental regulation. It rests on the assumption that states have a primary responsibility for the government of populations within their territories and puts aside the idea of government by a shifting network of overlapping systems of control.[9] At first, governmental regulation took the form of government by police, based on immanent knowledge of the population of a state, collected and gathered together in police manuals. However, government by police becomes too limited as soon as one sees society as self-regulating and as to be manipulated rather than organised. One must then, says Michel Foucault, take into account what it is. It becomes necessary to reflect upon it, upon its specific characteristics, its constants and variables. The rise of liberal government represents a shift to the more abstract and theoretical knowledge elaborated on the basis of what Foucault has termed 'the figure of man'. Because of its emphasis on individual liberty and on the self-regulating capacity of several domains of interaction in a population, liberal government involves knowledge of a different order. Important is Foucault's use of the term 'figure' rather than 'concept'. As Helliwell and Hindess (1999: 7) argue, the term does not refer to any one conception of the human individual; rather 'the figure of man' can take a variety of different forms within the constraints imposed by its ambiguous position as *both an object of knowledge and as a subject that knows*. As a consequence, the human being can be understood in various, even incompatible ways, but, at the same time, it appears invariably, say Helliwell and Hindess, 'as a creature of natural drives and appetites and also, unlike creatures of any other kind, as acting on the basis of *representations* he gives himself' (1999: 7, italics added). Helliwell and Hindess argue that the centrality of this figure in the human sciences explains the tenacity of concepts like culture, society, etc. which designate unities as defined or held together by shared understandings and values, and as independent, boundary-maintaining social systems. The figure of man underlies both the presumption of ideational unity and the presumption of systemic unity. It suggests, in particular, 'that human interaction should be seen as structured or regulated by shared representations, and so results in the pervasive use [in the human sciences] of "culture" and other such concepts to inscribe *sameness*' (1999: 9).

This pervasive use of 'culture' and similar concepts to inscribe sameness is a sign of what Zygmunt Bauman has named 'the ideology of culture'. Quoting de Tocqueville, he points out the revolutionary significance of those 'men of letters, men without wealth, social eminence, responsibilities, or official status', who 'became in practice the leading politicians of the age, since despite the fact that others held the reins of government, they alone spoke with authority' (Bauman 1987: 34). The significance is not that they took over the leadership of public opinion, says Bauman, but that they became a public in their *sociétés de pensée*, created public opinion and received for this creation an authority that enabled them to negotiate or compete with the power of those who held the reins of government. Their knowledge was power/knowledge that escaped the hands of the sovereign. However, the second slicing up of authority was possible only if this was not to the detriment of the state. In other words, though this slicing up opened a space for the self-regulating individual, it simultaneously forced the intellectuals studying this individual and its society into an (often troublesome) alliance with the state. The alliance was, however, sealed in a peculiar way. It was inscribed in the theories and intellectual visions themselves, though concealed by casting it in universal language. A central concept in this language was 'culture', a concept rooted in a particular vision of the world that legitimises the role of intellectuals. Three tacitly yet axiomatically accepted premises direct this vision:

> First, human beings are essentially incomplete and not self-sufficient. Their humanization is a process taking place after birth, in the company of other human beings. The distinction between the inherited insufficiency and acquired completeness is conceptualized as the opposition between 'biological' and 'social' aspects of the 'homo duplex,' or between 'nature' and 'nurture'. Second, humanization is essentially a learning process, split into the acquisition of knowledge and the taming, or repressing, of animal (and almost invariably antisocial) predispositions. The distinction between knowledge to be put in place of the natural predispositions and the predispositions it is to replace, is often conceptualized as the opposition between 'reason' and 'passions,' or between 'social norms' and 'instincts' or 'drives'. Third, learning is just one side of the relation of which the other side is teaching. The completion of the humanization process therefore requires teachers and a system of – formal or informal – education. The educators hold the key to the continuous reproduction of cohabitation as a human society. (Bauman 1989: 314)

The alliance turned intellectuals into claim makers from the start and involved them in processes in which they attempted with some degree of success to make these claims true in theory and in practice. Their grand design for a better society was, however, composed of what they knew best and were most satisfied with: their own mode of life. Their particular situation as an educated elite gave them the experience from which their new vision of the social world, as constituted by the learning/teaching activity, was extrapolated (Bauman 1989: 319). However, in the act of extrapolation, their intellectualistic position was projected upon those studied and raised as the universal norm for humanity. As a consequence, and thanks to the role of the intellectual as inscribed in their own theories and claims and their alliance with the state, a scholastic error is constantly made and remade not only in theory but also in practice. This not only led to a thorough secularisation (so deplored by Smith), but contributed in very complex and dynamic ways to our modern ways of living and living together. In what follows a minor part of this intricate tale is told.

'Religion', 'Society', 'Identity' and the Modern Liberal State

One such claim, made by intellectuals, is found in the concept of 'society'. Eric Wolf (1988) sees the concept as representing a claim, a claim advanced and enacted in order to construct a state of affairs that previously was not there. Society is an invention. The same can be said of religion as a sceptical political notion on which society as a claim and subsequent invented reality seems to depend. These are claims like those of nation, state and culture which, as Philip Corrigan and Derek Sayer argue in *The Great Arch* (1985), were 'used historically to organize and perpetuate rule and domination over oppositional groups anchored in different and variable pasts and experiences, to install new universalizing social and cultural identities in the course of cumulative revolutions in government' (Wolf 1988: 759). Seen from this perspective, society appears as a claim in a particular context and place. 'Its function announced itself as libertarian: to break the bonds of the past, to dismantle the connection between the macrocosm and kinship by the grace of God, and to assign dignity, autonomy, righteousness and rights to individuals, acting upon each other in pursuit of their interests' (ibid. 759). In a first instance it relied on building morality in the hearts of men; in a second step it aggressively used the state and law to shape the multitudes into conformity with the structures of morality. In the history of this particular invention, the notion of 'identity' is strongly implicated.

John D. Ely (1997) confirms the link between the notion of identity, which is pervasive in modern discourse, and the central *liberal* concepts of state and individual.[10] Ely shares the view of Zarka that Locke, and with him, Hume, developed the notion of personal identity out of the mathematical-metaphysical notion of identity by applying this and the mechanical paradigm of nature to psychology and jurisprudence of the state. He claims that the term has less to do with a civic, humanist orientation, than with the juridical subject philosophies most typically associated with liberalism. Locke uses a precise, nonqualitative, Euclidean framework, integrating the notion in a mechanical and law-driven and determinate philosophy of nature. The application of mechanical thinking contributes to putting aside a specifically civic republican concept of character development present in earlier modern philosophical tendencies to the advantage of the then emerging mercantile English state. As Zarka points out, Locke practically completes the transition from the Renaissance notion of *dignitas hominis*, containing a notion of man's own liberty to make of himself what he is and his responsibility to be what one becomes, to a notion of man as a being with rights without any dimension of becoming (Zarka 1999: 245). For Locke the juridical dimension is crucial if he wants to establish some independency for civil society. The possibility of this dimension asks for a particular being: a utilitarian self directed by pleasures and pains, rewards and punishments, and in possession of a personal identity to guarantee that one can be held responsible for one's own actions. Nevertheless, though Locke argues for personal liberty and civil government, at the same time he construes a self that becomes available for social engineering through a regime of behavioural conditioning. In other words, as Foucault argues, a space is opened up in which

people can become a subject in the two meanings of the word: 'subject to someone else by control and dependence; and tied to his own identity by a conscience or self-knowledge' (van der Veer 1996: 20). This newly constructed
inner space of personal identity, Ely (1997) argues, will become the site of
ascription by the state:

> The term is part of the state-building project of nationalism insofar as this utilizes
> *ascriptive* definitions of human beings strengthened and increasingly influential as
> the modern nation-state expands ... Ascription fits the character of the nation-state.
> It reflects the individual conceived increasingly as a member of an abstract or imag-
> ined community, mediated through a set of mechanical laws, rather than a face-to-
> face one. (Ely 1997: 74, 77)

An important contribution is made by John Stuart Mill, who elaborates on
Locke's malleable self and refines the concept of identity as part of a group psychology. He will use the term for the first time in its modern sense as national
identity. Eric Wolf's assertion that God came to be replaced with the Nation
finds its fulfilment here. In Mill's time, the idea of an identity of interests had
become increasingly important. It came to inform a notion of identity with a
sense of *ascriptive homogenisation*, referring no longer to the individuality of a
person but to that which is shared with others.

> Mill refers to those things that unite a portion of mankind as a nationality – 'common
> sympathies' that can be caused by the 'effects of identity of race and descent,' by
> 'community of language and community of religion, or by geographical limits.' But
> the strongest of all is identity of political antecedents: the possession of a national
> history, and consequent community of recollections; collective pride and humilia-
> tion, pleasure and regret, connected with the same incidents in the past. (Ely
> 1997: 79)

So, as the nation-state system is built, the term 'identity' increasingly becomes
associated with the idea of national identity. According to Ely, this association
reflects the interest of the late nineteenth- and early twentieth-century state in
identifying, cataloguing, measuring and regulating its subjects, its national
members, with modes of identification. He points in this regard to a paradox in
the term of identity.

> The individual identity in Locke's sense is always and everywhere utterly discrete. Yet
> the term develops in unmediated relation to the identity, the geographic and juris-
> dictional specificity, of a discrete national state. As a nation, and not as a constitu-
> tional form, this national unit remains as unique as the individual. The space
> between these two unmediated particularities will eventually be filled with emotions
> and feelings of national character, remaining thereafter remarkably impervious to
> rational comprehension ... (Ely 1997: 78)

Identity as a notion that emerged against the background of the development of
the modern state contains more than one paradox. As Ely just pointed out, it
refers, on the one hand, to what is unique to the individual; on the other hand,
it refers to what one has in common with others. A further contradiction can be
found, however, between identity as the inner space in which one is oneself sov-

ereign and identity as the ascriptively determined mode of defining individuals, ready for control and disciplining. Both contradictions are central to the project of the modern liberal state. In *The Great Arch* (1985), a study of the English state formation, Corrigan and Sayer concluded that the modern nation state leans heavily on the first two poles of identity: 'the individual and the nation, into which it "ceremonially inducts" students by utilizing systematic education':

> On the one hand, the state engages in a 'totalizing' project, representing all people as members of a national community. On the other hand, the state also tries to 'indi-vidualize' people in specific ways – as taxpayers, jurors, consumers, and yes, school-children. Through both of these 'disrupting' projects, alternative modes of collective and individual identification (and comprehension) ... are denied legitimacy. (Corrigan and Sayer 1985: 5)

In *Inventing Our Selves*, Nikolas Rose (1998) shows how the other two contrasting ideas of a free individual and a conditionable *tabula rasa* self became closely linked in the liberal project of the twentieth century. According to Rose, the modern liberal democracy became a possibility thanks to the human sciences that developed in the nineteenth and twentieth century. Typically, the free individual is very important for liberal democracy and so is the need to find a way of governing people without diminishing that freedom. The psychological sciences made the latter possible by devising techniques for the governance of oneself and for the guidance and education of those who had not yet reached that state of self-governance, or for those who had left it again. In other words, the psychological sciences have contributed to a regime of the self, in which each sees oneself as a self in development. Within this regime, concepts like freedom, autonomy and choice received a particular subjective character. The limits for conduct or for making choices are no longer imposed from the outside, by religious or political authorities, but now are found within the individual, who feels the need to develop his personality, to become someone and to discover who he really is:

> The forms of freedom we inhabit today are intrinsically bound to a regime of subjec-tification in which subjects are not merely 'free to choose', but *obliged to be free*, to understand and enact their lives in terms of choice under conditions that systemati-cally limit the capacities of so many to shape their own destiny ... Their choices are, in their turn, seen as realization of the attributes of the choosing self – expressions of personality – and reflect back upon the individual who has made them. (Rose 1998: 17)

Part of these practices of subjectification now is the project of discovering one's real identity, the identity, as Cantwell Smith would reply, one never seems to find.[11]

The entangled history of 'religion', 'society' and 'identity' outlined here, in which too little attention is given to the social processes and dynamics inform-ing and informed by these concepts as claims and to the active, nonnegligible part played by the subjects of the state, can only form a first step in carrying on the exercise Smith started. However, it lends enough material to elaborate the contrast between Cantwell Smith and Ninian Smart a little further, and to show the reasons behind their different attitudes towards the concept of 'identity'. I will argue that although both have been seen as exemplary for the liberal theological discourse within religious studies, Smart never left it. Smith, on the other hand, albeit with one foot out while looking historically at the subject matter, walked right into the trap again when thinking about how to improve the study of religion and subsequently got caught by the same dialectic he so eloquently described.

Cantwell Smith and Ninian Smart: Contrasted Again

Cantwell Smith, certain that the concept of religion was useless and led to distortions of the subject matter, developed new concepts and came up with a refreshing hypothesis about the relationship between us, human beings, and tradition. Without religious overtones, it could be stated as follows. Based on his findings of fundamental transitions in the meaning and use of terms such as 'belief', 'religion' and, more recently, 'holy scripture', he points out that a tradition is more than a mere compilation of ideas, values, rules and objects passed on from one generation to another as the content for one's world-view or identity, giving guidelines on how to live. Tradition is not a bunch of ideas and values one first interiorises and then implements. Neither is it ideas and beliefs supplemented with rituals, practices, art etc. which merely express those beliefs and meanings. Smith asks us to consider instead the hypothesis that the 'externalia' might be rather means in forms of human activity and learning that lead to results which are not in themselves transmittable from one person to another as beliefs and ideas are, but which are only accessible when going through the learning process oneself. Rather than seeing diversity as a matter of variation in beliefs, values and meanings, he suggests diversity is rather to be found in those activities and ways of learning. Smith also suggests that those means, such as texts, rosaries, stories, etc. do not completely determine the activity or the way of learning, nor the learning results. This means that merely studying these texts or objects will leave the most important part out of the picture: human activities and ways of learning. Smith's hypothesis allows for a way of learning in which one changes as a person, instead of merely piling up beliefs and values. Furthermore, he acknowledges that it does not need to be fully intentional. One does not necessarily set out to learn a particular something, an activity or a theory, but one finds oneself changing, transformed by certain activities, certain events. Intentionality is rather to be found as the search for such activities, such events, and in attempts to let others share in such experiences by giving them the means to learn and encouragement. Mostly misunderstood by others in the field of religious studies is the idea that externals are more than the mere expression of ideas and values and that learning results can be quite different from acquiring knowledge and beliefs, and can take a form in which it cannot be handed down directly, forcing each new generation to learn anew through personal transformations, sometimes minor, sometimes rather spectacular and not passing unnoticed. The difficulty lies in the fact that Smith casts his hypothesis in religious terms and talks about man's relationship to God. At this point, the awareness of opponents is raised. Does this talk of a relation to God not indicate that Smith – after all, of Protestant upbringing – assumes a sameness, an essence that reflects his own historical situatedness? Ninian Smart (1984), for instance, has expressed such ideas. In his opinion, Smith reduces the diversity in religious experiences as well as the many foci (gods, spirits, etc.) religion can have to only one – his own experience of the Christian God. This error is connected with the application of what Smart refers to as 'the Protestant principle'. The latter means that one lays too much stress on attitudes rather than outward actions. Smart is convinced, as are others, that Smith intends to narrow the study of religion to the study of 'faith' without much attention to the externalia, such as religious practices, religious art, doctrines, etc. Only the individual faith of the faithful would remain. In my opinion, however, the latter view is based on a misapprehension of Smith's ideas, although I agree that we should take seriously the accusation that his own Protestant background informs his ideas. Nevertheless, it is my opinion that his hypothesis lies outside the limits imposed by the figure of man. The presumption of an ideational unity needed to unite abstract individuals into one society is absent.

To place the argument within the model developed by Pinxten and Verstraete in the Introduction to this volume, Smith points towards a possibility of seeing tradition and religion not so much as solely belonging to the culturality dimension, but opens up a perspective of tradition as an element also in the personality and sociality dimensions. Smart, on the other hand, does not recognise the potentiality in Smith's work, misinterprets it and rejects it as theology because a specific Protestant position is universalised. At the same time, firmly stuck in liberal discourse, he approaches religion as in essence a matter of culturality, seeing 'identity' as a task. To him, everyone is a world-view constructor, in search of a meaningful framework in which one can situate oneself and give meaning to one's life. In this case, religious traditions give material or content, such as beliefs and values, to form an identity, an activity in which the religious person is actively engaged. This scenario can be criticised in several ways. Firstly, Smart appears as a school example of the very strong emphasis on meaning production in the Western Christian tradition. Secondly, he introduces a *sameness* that contains the presupposition of ideational unity and inscribes everyone in the modern search for an identity. Contrary to Smith's ideas, Smart sees each person as an abstract individual burdened with the task of searching for those ideas and values that will make a meaningful and peaceful life in coexistence possible. As such, he inscribes everyone in the liberal project in which individuals are obliged to be free in certain ways. Smart even devises a new international organisation, a World Academy of Religion, to enhance this project. McCutcheon, however, confirms these criticisms when he argues that the World Academy proposal relies on and promotes 'an utterly dysfunctional model of Religionswissenschaft, a model dependent upon a long tradition that misconceives scholarship on religion as simply comprising different species of the genus interreligious dialogue' (McCutcheon and Geertz 2000: 32).

Though Smith's ideas are interesting, the religious language in which he casts these, as well as his ideas about the study of religion and his project for a global theology discourage many from pursuing his line of thought. This is with good reason. In my opinion, these religious overtones show that he also commits what is a central mistake in the human sciences. Let me explain. Smith deplores the irreligiosity of the modern Western world and sees it as an important cause of many personal and social problems. Furthermore, he attributes the existing study of religion an important role in the secularisation of the West and wants to turn the tide. However, this does not mean that Smith puts science aside:

> as our culture has become increasingly permeated with what passes for a scientific outlook on knowledge and the world, and also on human matters, the increasing success in dealing with things has been accompanied, as everyone knows, with an increasing sickness of personal and social life: the depersonalization of social procedures, the fragmentation of community, the alienation of persons from their neighbour, from themselves, and from the world. As a humanist, I resist blaming this on science; I blame this on objectivization, misapplied from natural science to thinking about human affairs. (Smith and Burbidge 1997: 145)

Neither does Smith opt for the opposite and resist the notion 'that the only alternative to objectivity is subjectivism – a fallacy so loudly proclaimed that some believe it and therefore, fleeing from depersonalizing objectivity, turn to irrationality or even to drugs' (ibid. 145). Smith finds, however, material for an alternative in his empirical findings and suggests a humane study of religious and other human phenomena. But, apart from the many ambiguities in his proposal to learn as a human scientist humanely through personal transformations, reading this proposal for a humane science is like reading the draft for a new constitution in which, for moral reasons, the subject under study is given his share of authority:

> More egalitarianly, rather, I am suggesting that we have no Archimedean point. Our study must be collaborative. We must move beyond an interpretation from one perspective out on the others, to a human interpretation of all. A counterpart for the social sciences and humanities of the verificationist principle in the natural sciences is the principle that no statement about human affairs is true that cannot be existentially appropriated by those about whom the statement is made. Finally, no statement might be accepted as true that had not been inwardly appropriated by its author. Studies of that impersonalist kind whose truths make no difference to the moral character of the one who deals with them, would be rejected. (Smith and Burbidge 1997: 46)

In his draft for a new constitution, Smith argues for two things: he asks attention for the moral, personal side of human knowledge; and he argues that the existing deplorable situation can only be countered by giving a voice to the believers, the subjects under study themselves, in science, not only on the level of description but on the level of explanation or, in his case, humane comprehension as well. Both these elements are highly problematic. In outlining an alternative study of religion, Smith repeats the mistake made by those intellectuals caught in the ideology of culture by affirming the role of human science as it was inscribed in those theories and intellectual visions closely linked with the modern liberal state. In trying to create an equal partnership between those being studied and those studying in human science, Smith merely affirmed the previous constitution. Though he was very critical about the transformations that had taken place within Western society since the sixteenth and seventeenth centuries, and pointed to the harmful role of 'religion' as an outsider term that was part of an intellectualising and objectifying discourse, he nevertheless did not realise that the problem is not so much the concepts used in science as the role intellectuals inscribe for themselves in their theories. Smith's conclusion that the term 'religion' should be rejected for scientific use is again open for critical evaluation. Similarly, one cannot conclude, on the basis of the outlined history of religion, society and identity, that the latter concept should be dropped as well. Instead, attention should go to the way in which these concepts and theories contain traces of that original inscription which gave human science a place as well as a specific role in modern society. Another important task is given by Eric Wolf (1988: 760). He writes that 'we need to invent new ways of thinking about heterogeneity and the transformative nature of human arrangements' (although I am suspicious of his addition 'and to do so scientifically and humanistically at the same time'.) To conclude, the exercise Smith started, the unthinking of modernity, of the intellectualisation and infiltration of the outsider perspective in religious and other human practices, should be continued. This asks for a critical rethinking of the intellectual's role as it was originally inscribed and for new theorising about religion, society and identity outside of the ideology of culture.

Notes

1. Jonathan Z. Smith is another quite central scholar in religious studies, who is often quoted for his views on the concept of religion as a second-order term. In 'Religion, Religions, Religious' (1998) he paints a history which is at first sight quite compatible with Cantwell Smith's views. However, both see different implications for the study of religion and for the usefulness of the concept 'religion'. Whereas Cantwell Smith rejects the term for reasons explained further in this article, Jonathan Z. Smith sees no reason to do so but sees problems arising from confusing the second-order term religion with first-order phenomena.
2. The Christian Church saw itself as a *congregatio fidelium* or *universitas fidelium*, a congregation in which the members were connected to each by common 'fides' and, based on this, by obedience to common law (Molnar 2002).
3. Sir Robert Filmer developed such ideas in his *Patriarcha or the Natural Power of Kings*, and was directly attacked for these by John Locke in his *Two Treatises of Government* (1690).
4. '[C]e qui réapparaît au moment où le gouvernement est dissous, c'est un corps souverain animé d'une volonté unique et habilité à interpréter la loi de nature, et non pas une série de consciences individuelles ... la société ... peut subsister, avec ses rapports d'obligation juridique qui lient les individus envers les décisions de la majorité, lorsque le gouvernement a disparu' (Spitz 1993: 62–63).
5. A more recent example of this heritage of 'religion' as a sceptical concept referring to common values and seen as necessary for the existence of society can be found with Durkheim, an important figure in sociology and anthropology. He saw his 'religion of humanity' as an inte-

grative force. Of course, by that time some fundamental changes had occurred and it was not without reason that Durkheim ascribed the public school an important role in bringing about moral greatness (Wallace 1977: 289). As he said in an article about the school of tomorrow: 'It is necessary to have respect for legitimate authority, that is to say, for moral authority, to inculcate in the child the *religion* of law, and to teach him the joy of acting in concert with others according to an impersonal, universal law. It is necessary that the school discipline appear to the children as a just and sacred thing, the basis of their happiness and moral health. Thus as men they will accept spontaneously and with open eyes the social discipline which cannot be undermined without endangering the whole social fabric' (ibid.).

6.   Lionel Trilling has pointed out, according to Webb Keane (1997: 682), that the development of the concept of sincerity is linked to that of 'society' as something that is separate from, and can become a discursive object for, the free individual (see Trilling 1972).

7.   The 'a' is emphasised to make clear that this process does not entail the coming about of a reality exactly as it was claimed by philosophers and human scientists. One should keep in mind that although changes in society are not a mere result of changing ideas, ideas, theories and human science nevertheless had a particular impact.

8.   Locke himself, however, saw society simply as a matter of flux, which could not be 'known' in any sense related to dominant contemporary conceptions of social knowledge (McClure 1990: 384).

9.   The Treaty of Westphalia in 1648 is a landmark in this development. It tried to make an end to sectarian religious slaughter in Germany in part by assigning to states the responsibility for the management of religious affairs within their territories. It restricted the rights of participating states to intervene in each other's affairs in matters of religion. As such it secured conditions in which states could begin to develop long-term and comprehensive strategies for the government of their respective populations. C. Larner points to Christianity as the first political ideology replacing older kinship and feudal ties (Corrigan and Sayer 1985: 47).

10. A genealogy of the term (identity), reveals that the two most important sources of the term's meanings are perspectives that generally stand opposed to both communitarianism and multiculturalism. One important source is British empiricism, with John Locke as central figure; another important source is dialectic and can be found with Hegel.

11. Another aspect of this project is the task of identification. This idea of identity, developed in the nineteenth century with Freud as an important contributor, was popularised by Erik Erikson in 1960s. As Ely points out, the state is present here as well. 'The term is developed by Erikson as a way to address perceived difficulties of immigrants assimilating in a majority culture and thus retains its central role in managing state-building via ascription' (Ely 1997: 82–86).

Bibliography

Asad, Talal. 1996. 'Comments on Conversion'. In *Conversion to Modernities: The Globalization of Christianity*, ed. Peter van der Veer, 263–73. London: Routledge.

Bauman, Zygmunt. 1987. *Legislators and Interpreters*. Cambridge: Polity Press.

———— 1989. 'Legislators and Interpreters. Culture as Ideology of Intellectuals'. In *Social Structure and Culture. Part II: Culture and Modernity*, ed. Hans Haferkamp, 313–32. Berlin: Walter de Gruyter & Co.

Corrigan, Philip and Sayer, Derek. 1985. *The Great Arch: English State Formation as Cultural Revolution*. Oxford: Basil Blackwell.

Ely, John D. 1997. 'Community and the Politics of Identity. Toward the Genealogy of a Nation-State Concept', *Stanford Humanities Review*, Vol. 5, No. 2: 70–95. http://www.stanford.edu/group/SHR/5-2/elly.html

Gellner, Ernest. 1987. *Culture, Identity and Politics*. Cambridge: Cambridge University Press.

Goyard-Fabre, Simone. 1988. 'Pouvoir Juridictionnel et Gouvernement Civil dans la Philosophie Politique de Locke', *Revue Internationale de Philosophie*, Vol. 42: 192–214.

Helliwell, Christine and Hindess, Barry. 1999. ' "Culture", "Society" and the Figure of Man', *History of the Human Sciences*, Vol. 12, No. 4: 1–20.

Idinopulos, Thomas A. 1998. 'What is Religion?', *Cross Currents*, Vol. 48, No. 3: 366–80. http://www.crosscurrents.org/whatisreligion.htm

Keane, Webb. 1997. 'From Fetishism to Sincerity. On Agency, the Speaking Subject, and their Historicity in the Context of Religious Conversion', *Comparative Studies in Society and History*, Vol. 39, No. 4: 674–93.

Latour, Bruno. 1990. 'Postmodern? No, simply Amodern! Steps towards an Anthropology of Science', *Studies in the History of the Philosophy of Science*, Vol. 21, No. 1: 145–71.

Locke, John. 1690. *An Essay Concerning the true Original, Extent, and End of Civil Government*. Converted to HTML by J.A. Donald: http://jim.com/2ndtreat.htm

MacIntyre, Alasdair. 1969. 'The Fate of Theism'. In *The Religious Significance of Atheism*, eds. Alasdair MacIntyre and Paul Ricoeur, 3–29. New York: Columbia University Press.

Martin, Luther H. 2000. 'Review Symposium on Russell T. McCutcheon's Manufacturing Religion. The Discourse on Sui Generis Religion', *Culture and Religion*, Vol. 1: 95–97.

McCutcheon, Russell T. 1997. *Manufacturing Religion. The Discourse on Sui Generis Religion and the Politics of Nostalgia*. New York: Oxford University Press.

———— and Geertz, Armin R. 2000. 'The Role of Method and Theory in the IAHR', *Method and Theory in the Study of Religion*, Vol. 12: 3–37.

McClure, Kristie M. 1990. 'Difference, Diversity, and the Limits of Toleration', *Political Theory*, Vol. 18, No. 3: 361–91.

Molnar, Attila. 2002. 'The Construction of the Notion of Religion in Early Modern Europe', *Method and Theory in the Study of Religion*, Vol. 14: 47–60.

Parry, Geraint. 1998. 'The Sovereign as Educator. Thomas Hobbes's National Curriculum', *Paedagogica Historica*, Vol. 34, No. 3: 711–30.

Preus, Samuel. 1987. *Explaining Religion: Criticism and Theory from Bodin to Freud*. New Haven, Conn.: Yale University Press.

Reynolds, Noel B. and Saxonhouse, Arlene W. (eds.) 1995. *Thomas Hobbes. Three Discourses*. Chicago, Ill.: University of Chicago Press.

Rose, Nikolas. 1998. *Inventing Our Selves*. Cambridge: Cambridge University Press.

Shapin, Steven and Schaffer, Simon. 1985. *Leviathan and the Air-pump: Hobbes, Boyle, and the Experimental Life*. Princeton, N.J.: Princeton University Press.

Smart, Ninian. 1984. 'Scientific Phenomenology and Wilfred Cantwell Smith's Misgivings'. In *The World's Religious Traditions: Current Perspectives in Religious Studies*, ed. Frank Whaling, 257–69. Edinburgh: T. & T. Clark Ltd.

———— 1992. 'W.C. Smith and Complementarity', *Method and Theory in the Study of Religion*, Vol. 4, No. 1–2: 20–26.

Smith, Jonathan Z. 1982. *Imagining Religion: From Babylon to Jonestown*. Chicago, Ill.: University of Chicago Press.

———— 1998. 'Religion, Religions, Religious'. In *Critical Terms for Religious Studies*, ed. Mark C. Taylor, 269–84. Chicago, Ill.: University of Chicago Press.

Smith, Wilfred Cantwell. 1962. *The Meaning and End of Religion*. London: SPCK.

————1979. *Faith and Belief*. Princeton, N.J.: Princeton University Press.

———— and Oxtoby, Willard G. 1982. *Religious Diversity*. New York, N.Y.: Crossroad.

——— and Burbidge, John (eds.) 1997. *Modern Culture from a Comparative Perspective*. Albany: State University of New York Press.

Spitz, Jean-Fabien. 1993. 'Concept de Souveraineté et Politique placée sous le Signe de la Loi de Nature dans le *Second Traité du Gouvernement Civil* de Locke. *Philosophie*, Vol. 37: 39–63.

Stout, Jeffrey. 1981. *The Flight from Authority. Religion, Morality and the Quest for Autonomy*. Notre Dame, Ind.: University of Notre Dame Press.

Surin, Kenneth. 1990a. 'Towards a "Materialist" Critique of Religious Pluralism. An Examination of the Discourse of John Hick and Wilfred Cantwell Smith'. In *Religious Pluralism and Unbelief. Studies Critical and Comparative*, ed. Ian Hamnett, 114–29. London: Routledge.

——— 1990b. 'A Certain "Politics of Speech". "Religious Pluralism" in the Age of the McDonald's Hamburger', *Modern Theology*, Vol. 7, No. 1: 67–100.

Trilling, Lionel. 1972. *Sincerity and Authenticity*. London: Oxford university Press.

van der Veer, Peter (ed.) 1996. *Conversion to Modernities: The Globalization of Christianity*. London: Routledge.

Wallace, Ruth A. 1977. 'Emile Durkheim and the Civil Religion Concept', *Review of Religious Research*, Vol. 18: 287–90.

Wiebe, Donald. 1991. 'From Religious to Social Reality. The Transformation of "Religion" in the Academy', *Scottish Journal of Religious Studies*, Vol. 12: 127–38.

Wolf, Eric R. 1988. 'Inventing Society', *American Ethnologist*, Vol. 15: 752–61.

Zarka, Yves Charles. 1993. 'Identité et Ipséité chez Hobbes et Locke', *Philosophie*, Vol. 37: 5–19.

——— 1999. 'The Invention of the Subject of the Law', *British Journal for the History of Philosophy*, Vol. 7, No. 2: 245–62.

2

ENGENDERING IDENTITIES AS POLITICAL PROCESSES: DISCOURSES OF GENDER AMONG STRICTLY ORTHODOX JEWISH WOMEN

Chia Longman

Identity and Gender: Analytical or Political Concepts? Some Theoretical Excursions

At first sight the concept of identity would appear to be central to the theorisation of gender, as it can be understood as the – however temporary – sedimentation of the process of establishing sameness through difference, of identification through differentiation along an axis of sex/gender. It could equally be argued that sexual difference may be a primary marker and perhaps the universal ground for what appears to be one of the most fundamental distinctions in identities, that of women and men. However, neither gender nor identity have ever been straightforward analytical concepts, convenient tools for capturing and then representing complex individual, social or cultural phenomena, yet heavily invested with multiple meanings. Usages of both concepts are furthermore tied to political stakes, most notably from the perspective of recent feminist theorising.

Early attempts to theorise notions of gender and gender identity have meanwhile been taken to task for their implicit essentialist presuppositions. Among these have been the dominance of biological deterministic schemes of thought, the inability to think beyond dichotomies such as nature/culture, men/women, and both the conflation of and assumed relationships between ambiguous notions of sex, gender, sexuality, including the meanings of terms such as sexual or gender identity and roles. Psychiatrist Robert Stoller's introduction of the concept of gender identity brought with it an attempt to question such biological determinism by delineating sex as biological from gender as a term with 'psychological and cultural rather than biological connotations' (from *Sex and Gender* published in 1968, in Oakley 1996: 159). In hindsight, although this distinction has become commonplace within contemporary gender studies, its application nonetheless remains far from universal or unproblematic. For example, in referring to the sex and gender terminology during the period of the popular quantitative research into 'the psychology of sex differences' and the so-called masculinity–femininity tests on personality and behavioural characteristics of the 1970s, Katchadourian (1979: 25) already comments on the 'promiscuous' use of such terms as sexual or gender identity and sexual or gender role. Not only does there appear to exist confusion about the biological as opposed to the cultural in terms of explanation, but also confusion about what, then, was to be perceived as the close relationship between identity and role: subjective feelings, the perception of the self and cognition, on the one hand, versus social status, location and behaviour, linked to societal expectations and labels, on the other.

Later, many important new feminist theories of the acquisition of individual gender identity would in fact draw on classic psychoanalytic thought. Examples are the object-relations theory of Nancy Chodorow (1978) and French post-structuralist Lacanian theories of sexual difference, with figures such as Luce Irigaray and Julia Kristeva. Despite the emphasis of the latter on systems of meaning and the symbolic order, their exposure of the Cartesian, masculine unitary subject, and the insistence on the constructed nature of femininity and masculinity by both schools of thought, however, these theories have not been widely applied in the research of gender in cross-cultural and comparative contexts. Socialisation theories of gender that focus on the way the individual acquires a social gender identity and relates to other gendered individuals have, then again, been criticised on the grounds of their neglect for individual variance, the role of the unconscious and often their reductionism of power relations to the mere description of the social roles assigned to women and men (Brouns 1995: 55, Scott 1996: 156). From the perspective of many feminist postmodern critiques, all these variants of feminist theories have often been accused for their 'metanarrative overtones', including their essentialist and universalistic accounts of gender identity and other categories such as sexuality, reproduction and mothering (Fraser and Nicholson 1990, Weir 1996). Another major critique has been directed at their insistence on the primacy and originary nature of binary sexual difference (Butler 1990a, Moore 1994b).

Research outside of contemporary Western society has not only produced empirical material that questions what can be perceived as the binary opposition between male and female that underlies these theories (see below). It has also contributed to the development of the idea that gender is socially or culturally constructed in culturally variable ways. Individual gender identity can therefore be understood as culturally constructed in the anthropological sense, in that societies in space and time differ in their definitions of masculinity or femininity, as argued *avant-la-lettre* by Margaret Mead (1963, orig. 1935) of course, and later in many important contributions in the field of feminist anthropology since the 1970s (e.g., Martin and Voorhies 1975, Ortner and Whitehead 1981, Sanday and Goodenough 1990). This cultural dimension of gender – referring to the level of widely used concepts such as gender constructs, gender ideology, gender symbolism, or gender meanings – in particular in relation to power, has ever since been the primary focus of much feminist research, precisely in the necessary emphasis against biological essentialist and therefore potentially politically determinative explanations of social inequalities between women and men. In the remains of this introduction I will make some brief points about what I see as some interrelated shifts in our understanding of gender and identity, which can be viewed as much broader than the theorising of the coherent concept of individual gender identity per se, as briefly characterised above.

Gender/Difference

First of all, the concept of gender has grown to be an interdisciplinary and encompassing category of analysis which transcends the mere level of the individual and the family, in order to study its relationship to subtle and structural inequalities embedded in social and political relationships, institutions, symbolic systems, etc. As proposed in an influential essay by the feminist historian Joan Scott (1996: 167), gender can be seen as 'a constitutive element of social relationships based on perceived differences between the sexes'. Secondly – influenced by Michel Foucault – Scott (1996: 169) claims that gender, power and politics are related in the sense that 'gender is a primary field within which or by means of which power is articulated'. The first proposition involves four interrelated elements, firstly that of symbols or symbolic representations. A second element includes normative concepts 'that set forth interpretations of the meanings of the symbols, that attempt to limit and contain their metaphoric possibilities'. Thirdly, there is the level of social institutions and organisations, from kinship systems to the political arena, and finally that of subjective identity.[1] Scott furthermore argues that this analytical model of gender construction can equally serve in discussions of class, race, ethnicity, etc. More than just subject matter, Scott's model is but one prominent example of how gender has become something of a heuristic device or a lens through which to look and critically study much more than, for instance, the psychological conflicts within or between individuals. It throws light on the general question of difference and power within society and ideology, and how these come to be institutionalised as structural patterns and practices of inequality between women and men, themselves engendered through cultural ideologies of sexual difference.

As alluded to above, the shift in focus from the individual to include the social and the cultural has also been accompanied by a questioning of the usefulness and universal accuracy of a distinction between sex as biological and gender as cultural, and the essentialism this dichotomy does reproduce. Feminist anthropologists Sylvia Yanagisako and Jane Collier (1987, 1990) and Henrietta Moore (1993, 1994a, 1994b, 1999) have asserted this binary model may be no more than simply part of Western folk ideology. What may have been perceived to be liberatory, from the perspective of feminist theory, thus turns out to be ethnocentric, and ultimately equally essentialist. No matter how culturally constructed gender is viewed, according to this model it always functions as 'the social elaboration in specific contexts of the obvious facts of biological sex difference' (Moore 1994b: 12). From a somewhat different, but nonetheless more influential angle, feminist theories have been strongly influenced by Judith Butler's (1990a) poststructuralist refutation of the sex/gender distinction. Butler (1990a: 7) questions whether the 'natural facts of sex' are themselves the product of various discourses in the service of particular political interests, arguing that sex is as culturally constructed as gender, the latter being the 'discursive/cultural means by which "sexed nature" or "a natural sex" is produced and established as "prediscursive"'.

Another important shift in the de-essentialising and de-individualising of the concept of gender can be detected in what appears to be a convergence between feminist social scientific and more poststructuralist and postmodern theoretical approaches. Here, the focus of analysis is moved from the deconstruction of sex/gender categories to the process of the construction of gender and embodiment itself, the (en)gendering, as it were. Whether this focus on the practice or performance of gender is located in discursive strategies or in the dynamic social processes or projects that constitute and in turn are constituted by gender structures (Ferree et al. 1999: xxxiii), gender is to be seen as a result or temporary effect of the 'doing gender' itself (West and Zimmerman 1987). Examples of this convergence are Morris's (1995) account of the impact of performance theory on the anthropology of sex and gender and Sered's (1998, 1999) ethnographical research into societies that lack explicit gender ideologies, despite the presence of gender roles and gendered ritual practice.

Identity/Sameness

These anti-essentialist approaches towards gender hold for the notion of identity in a similar deconstructive mode. Identity may function to displace the primacy of gender into 'more complex conceptions of social identity, treating gender as one relevant strand among others, attending also to class, race, ethnicity, age and sexual orientation' (Fraser and Nicholson 1990: 34–35). However, in recent feminist theorising, identity does not function as an analytical concept in quite the same way as gender, however problematic – theoretically or politically – the latter might be. The notion of identity has been problematised in conjunction with the category of 'women' as questionable rather than self-evident or foundational concepts grounding feminist political projects (e.g., Butler 1990a, 1990b, Riley 1988, 1992). In questioning the unitary notion of 'woman' or – in the plural and as a social group – 'women' as ontological categories of fixed and stable identity, pleas have been made for a radical critique or indeed a total subversion of identity itself as the primary goal of feminist politics (Butler 1990a). In such a feminist poststructuralist approach, gender identity is seen as a product of domination and oppression, constituted through symbolic systems or institutions of power (Weir 1996). As a political category, any form of identity is therefore seen as suspect, as it constantly risks fixation, constriction, essentialism and reification within what has been termed identity politics, where one's politics are based on a sense of personal and shared identity. As Butler (1992: 15–16) argues, identity can never function as a point of departure for feminist political practice, as 'identity categories are never merely descriptive, but always normative, and as such, exclusionary'.

More central to recent feminist theory have been the notions of the subject and subjectivity (e.g., Braidotti 1994). These may offer the possibility of conceiving agency without the objectification that is involved in the attribution of categories of identity, such as that of 'woman'. Moore (1994b) argues that anthropology is in need of such a theory of the subject as is applied in poststructuralist feminist theory. Despite anthropology's emphasis on the cultural variability of constructions of gender, Moore (1994b: 54–55) argues that gender identity is often merely seen as an outcome of the exposure and socialisation into such cultural categories. This leads to an impossibility of a theorisation of the process of the acquisition and reproduction of gender identity as such. Opposed to the modern idea of the unitary subject, the rational – supposedly ungendered – individual as the locus for action and thought, feminist poststructuralist theory proposes the idea of the internally differentiated subject, made of multiple and contradictory positionings and subjectivities. Individuals can be seen as 'multiply constituted subjects', who take up multiple 'subject positions' within a range of hegemonic and less dominant discourses and social practices on femininity and masculinity, whilst reproducing or resisting these. As Moore remarks, this theory of the subject is not without its own problems in terms of analysis, especially in understanding how and why certain acts of reproduction and resistance, compliance, etc. take place. However, it does offer theoretical ideas and some methodological tools on how to study gender identity in a nonessentialist way, taking into account all levels from the symbolic, to the institutional, practical and the internally contradictory subjective level of the individual. A focus on positionings or locations furthermore allows for a more intersectional perspective of identity, one in which markers of identity and difference such as gender, ethnicity, class, etc. exist in complex interrelationships and hierarchies with each other and are not reified into 'abstract universals' (Alcoff and Potter 1993: 3).

In the following analysis I will be drawing on some of these theorisations of gender and identity in the discussion of my own and existing research on women in strictly Orthodox Jewish communities. Methodologically, the idea of subject positionings is applied in the context of the research relationship and the interactive process of qualitative interviewing. The focus thereby is on the subject positions taken regarding gender, expressing and in relation to various discourses ('natural', religious, political) on the differences between women and men. Gender as an analytical device is used in order to make two main arguments on the relationship between gender and identity with regard to different strictly Orthodox Jewish communities. Additionally, it is suggested that links and comparisons are to be drawn between these and other kinds of traditionalist or fundamentalist movements. These two arguments show how gender, itself multifaceted and as an analytical concept, then functions at different levels in the multidimensional model of identity proposed by Pinxten and Verstraete in the Introduction to this volume. In this sense, and as the editors argue, identity is not rejected, but reclaimed as an instrument of critical analysis into the workings of essentialist claims.

First I will compare two different forms of Orthodox Jewish female identity. Next to a reading of Davidman's (1991) and Kaufman's (1993) studies of *ba'alot teshuvah* in the U.S. (that is, secular women who have 'returned' to Orthodox Judaism at some stage of their lives), I will be making a comparison drawing on my own interviews with 'frum-born' women belonging to the strictly Orthodox Jewish community of Antwerp, Belgium. In terms of the editors' model of identity, I suggest that for the former group, individual gender identity is paramount and imbued with cultural and religious meanings (the dimension of culturality). In contrast, in the particular 'positionings' of the women in my own case study, ethnic/religious identification appeared more relevant than gender, itself more of a question of roles and practice, thus determined by the dimension of sociality. In the second place, I wish to argue how gender can be understood to apply to more than just the level of individual identity, as it proves crucial for the construction and reproduction of the identity of the group or community. As has been shown to be the case for many religious traditionalist, fundamentalist and nationalist groups in the contemporary world, both the actual control of women's behaviour and the symbolic elevation of women as 'bearers of the collective' (Yuval-Davis 1997) often turn out to be cross-cultural features of the identity politics of these movements. As similarly became apparent in my own interviews with strictly Orthodox Jewish women, gender is both dynamic and functions as an important boundary marker in the historical and actual process of constructing the own identity versus that of the other.

Strictly Orthodox Jewry: Labels and Genealogies

In recent years new labels and self-labels have come to replace what was usually referred to as 'ultra-Orthodox Jewry'. The 'ultra-Orthodox' are those contemporary religious Jewish men and women who are considered traditionalist in that they differ from both non-Jews and other secular and religious Jews (including the modern Orthodox) 'by the way of their dress, attitudes, worldview, and the character of their religious life' (Heilman and Friedman 1991: 197). 'Orthodox' in general has functioned as a label for religious Jews who continue to follow and practise Jewish law (*halakhah*) according to the rabbinical tradition. From the Orthodox point of view, halakhic Judaism is the only way to conceive of Judaism as a religion, in contrast to modern 'denominations' such as Reform, and later Conservative or Liberal Judaism that developed in the context of modernisation, assimilation and the Haskalah (Jewish Enlightenment), against the background of the major political and societal changes that took place in eighteenth- and nineteenth-century Europe.

Scholars reluctant to use the label 'ultra-Orthodox' – a construction by outsiders rather than a native concept – for referring to what appear to be the most religiously observant and contra-acculturative Jewish communities, have argued that the term *haredi* is more appropriate. Heilman (1992: 12) suggests the biblically derived term *haredim*, 'those who tremble (at the word of the Lord)', first applied in modern Hebrew, is better suited in referring to traditionalist Jews. It is not clear in any of the recent literature though, to what extent the term is used by both insiders and outsiders outside of Israel, in the many diasporic traditionalist communities of Jews that currently thrive in various places all over the world. Webber (1994: 27) uses the label 'strictly Orthodox' when referring to haredi, seemingly more adequate as a purely descriptive name, yet carrying less pejorative connotations than ultra-Orthodox. As Webber (1987, 1997) has emphasised, all categories of identifying particular groupings and communities are relative as well as dynamic in their appropriation and internalisation both by outsiders and amongst insiders themselves, dependent on and always in relationship with contexts of complex historical and sociological shifts.

One name that is used both internationally and in the self-description of an important segment of traditionalist religious Jews is 'Hasidic' (singular: a Hasid (male) or Hasidista (female) or plural, the Hasidim). Hasidism is furthermore used as both an insider and an outsider generic category in referring both to a religious tradition and the identity of a type of community. Hasidism – translated as piety – can be considered a religious movement with roots dating back to the seventeenth century in Eastern Europe. In this respect, Hasidism, as a religious tradition with a historical genealogy and a tangible institutional continuity to the present, predates 'Orthodoxy', which only developed towards the end of the nineteenth century in the context of complete assimilation, or the readaptation of Jewish religious practice to modern society. However, not all contemporary traditionalist or strictly Orthodox Jews identify as Hasidic, partly because of some earlier historical developments.

The Hasidic movement developed during the seventeenth century in a climate of political and economic hardship for the Jewish communities in Poland, White Russia and the Ukraine, next to a spiritual crisis for the poor masses who were ignored by rabbinic scholars and authorities. Folk religion with an emphasis on mysticism, ritual and devotion to charismatic leadership became popular in these surroundings, a stark contrast to the rabbinical understanding of piety as the intellectual study and learning of the law. One of the many charismatic mystical preachers of these times became known as *Besht* (Baal Shem Tov or Master of the Good Name), who gathered many disciples during the first half of the eighteenth century. Additional Hasidic movements developed all over Eastern Europe and after the death of the Besht, Hasidism spread even further and became institutionalised in terms of its teachings and structure, with the introduction of a form of leadership in the figure of the *rebbe*, a holy person whose authority was based on his piety and charisma.

Before the development of different Hasidic courts, each following their own personal rebbe, the movement encountered great opposition from rabbinic authorities, especially when it reached Lithuania. These opponents, the Misnagdim, rejected the cult surrounding the rebbe and the emphasis on spirituality and mysticism, by remaining committed to the priority of both law and Torah study. In the nineteenth century the differences between the Hasidim and the Misnagdim began to diminish. Hasidic courts and dynasties developed, taking their name from the town or community in which they were originally based, such as the Satmar in Hungary, the Belz in Galicia, the Lubavitch (also known as Chabad) in Russia, etc. The Misnagdic rebbe, the *rav*, was eventually attributed similar characteristics as the rebbe, such as charisma as well as scholarly authority (Heilman and Friedman 1991: 210), although the centrality and authority of the yeshiva remained great.

Hasidim and Misnagdim both refused to succumb to the growing forces of secularisation and modernisation following the Enlightenment and the French Revolution that finally began to seep into Eastern Europe in the twentieth century, adamantly resisting assimilation or other forms of acculturation that were taking place among many European Jews. It seems quite ironic that, according to Heilman and Friedman (1991: 208), Hasidism could be viewed as a revolutionary movement of its time. For 'from the perspective of modernity' more than two centuries later, Hasidim are held to be the most stubborn resisters to the liberatory changes taking place in the surrounding society. They refused to acculturate in order to preserve their unique – and what they see as the only authentic – way of Jewish life. In any case, by the beginning of the twentieth century, Hasidism similarly took on aspects of Misnagdism, such as the emphasis on Torah study and yeshiva learning, which today function as central to the strictly Orthodox Jewish lifestyle, typical of the highly gendered 'scholars' society' of religious men fulfilling their halakhic obligation of daily study and prayer.

The Eastern European Hasidic and Misnagdic Jews and their rebbes that survived the Holocaust mostly emigrated to the U.S. and Israel, where weak forms of Orthodoxy had existed prior to the Second World War and which sometimes became 'hasidified' under the impact of the traditionalist newcomers. The Hasidim, Misnagdim (or what are now called the haredim or strictly Orthodox Jews) not only continue to refuse assimilation or acculturation to modern secular society. They also endeavour to abide by halakhah and to practise their religious traditions and customs, speaking Yiddish, living and dressing as they did in the East European *shtetls* (small Jewish towns in Eastern Europe) town all those centuries ago. Settlements of descendants of Hasidic Eastern European Jewry are to be found, for example, in the New York areas of Brooklyn, such as the Satmar in Williamsburg, or the Lubavitcher in Crown Heights; and in the Mea Shearim area of Jerusalem or Bnei Barak outside of Tel Aviv. These diasporic communities themselves are vastly international and migratory, with, for example, arranged marriages taking place between followers of the same court from different countries, reaching to European cities such as London (Stamford Hill) and Paris, but also smaller towns and places, as far away as Australia, South America and South Africa.[2]

Hasidistas and Other Strictly Orthodox Jewish Women as Religious Agents

Contemporary social scientific studies of Hasidic communities have not only been few in number, but, according to Belcove-Shalin (1995a), they have also been guided by the secularisation or modernisation thesis, at least until the

1970s in the sociology and ethnography of religion.[3] It was expected that the trend of Judaism developing further into a 'civil religion' would persist. The majority would simply become secular and assimilate into the surrounding society, apart from a minority of religious Jews opting for Progressive redefinitions of Judaism, such as Conservative and Reform, who had accommodated religious belief and practice to the Christian model as dominant in Western society. To date, ethnographic studies of Hasidic communities have still been limited in number, but are less doubtful as to their survival and steady growth. The best-known ethnographical work has predominantly focused on the U.S. and Canada (see the contributions and numerous references in Belcove-Shalin 1995b), followed by a smaller number of more recent studies on or including the haredim in Israel (e.g., El-Or 1994, Heilman 1992, Landau 1993, Meijers 1992). Finally, ethnographical studies of strictly Orthodox Jewish communities in Europe appear to be even rarer, with exceptions such as Jacques Gutwirth's research on the Belzer Hasidim in Antwerp (1968, 1970) and Harry Rabinowicz's more historical account of the Hasidim in Britain.[4]

From the perspective of gender, the social scientific study of strictly Orthodox Jewry can be characterised by yet another feature: the invisibility of women as ethnographic subjects. One way to account for this lacuna is the actual exclusion of Orthodox Jewish women from the public institutional sphere of religious practice, opposed to what at first sight appears to be their more peripheral or at least more private forms of religious practice as prescribed by traditional patriarchal religious discourse and law. On the other hand, as feminist critiques of epistemology and methodology in recent decades have shown, no matter how patriarchal or androcentric a society or social setting may appear, this does not warrant the invisibility of women or their treatment as the 'other', or a mere object of religious discourse. These critiques hold for both the research process (e.g., only interviewing men or men on women) and ethnographic representation and theory formation in general, where the male norm – e.g., *homo religiosus* – is often taken to be, or represented as, the human norm (e.g., Bynum 1986, Gross 1977, Harding 1986, 1991, King 1995, Stacey and Thorne 1998, Stanley and Wise 1990).

In gender-conservative – and to a great extent gender-segregated – communities such as the strictly Orthodox, cultural and religious norms circumscribing the possibilities of interaction between women and men are often extrapolated to contacts with outsiders. This has also been – although not always explicitly acknowledged – an important factor in accounting for the invisibility of women within ethnographic research and representation, as it has severely complicated or even prevented access to women for male researchers. According to the traditionalist interpretation of halakhah, women must not be alone with men other than their husbands. Male ethnographers have therefore been limited in their access to the private sphere of the home. They have had little chance of researching women's more private and 'intimate' rituals, such as those pertaining to the laws of family purity, which even amongst the strictly Orthodox themselves are not discussed publicly. In any case, as a type of community circumscribed by such a patriarchal dualistic model of gender – as in

Joan Scott's model – at the level of both ideology, institutional arrangements and individual identity, the perspective of gender also shows how the identity and positioning of the researcher may deeply affect methodology and the outcomes of any research.

Religious law, expressed in the *mitzvot* – the positive and negative precepts the traditionalist observant Jew must abide by or perform – does not limit itself to public institutionalised religious rituals such as prayer and Talmud study for men, or ceremonial rites of passage such as at birth, bar mitzvah for boys, marriage, etc., which have often been the main subject of many ethnographies of Hasidim. It includes also regulations on all aspects of everyday life, from eating (the laws of kashrut), to washing, dressing, etc. Patriarchal tradition and religious discourse furthermore prescribes gendered behaviour and rituals, which has specific consequences for women's religious role, particularly in terms of their mothering and domestic obligations, but also the most private or intimate spheres of life such as reproduction and sexuality. In many traditionalist Orthodox Jewish communities to date, women remain exempt from the religious duty to practise commandments such as Talmud study,[5] the wearing of *tefillin* and *tzitzit*[6] during prayer (including the daily recitation of the Shema prayer), dwelling in a sukah (booth) on Sukkot (Feast of the Tabernacles), the hearing of the shofar on Rosh Hashanah (at the beginning of Yom Kippur) and other religious rituals which can all be seen as paradigmatic – male – religious public practice. The rationale usually put forward for women's exemption from these positive precepts is that they are ritual obligations which are bound to fixed times, the performance of which could interfere with their primary responsibility for familial and domestic tasks within the home. Through the sacralisation of all aspects of life, the domestic sphere is nonetheless seen as important for the continuation of religious tradition. It is here that the woman prepares food according to the religious dietary laws, and is held responsible for the primary religious education of the very young before they go to school. However, women do not partake in the typical scholars' society and cannot hold official religious functions and positions of authority such as rabbi or judge. Nor do they enjoy parallel rites of passage, such as the well-known bar mitzvah ceremony, which marks the male transition to religious adulthood and responsibility.

Apart from this role as an 'enabler' who makes sure the husband can fulfil his religious duties, there are three positive mitzvot which are exclusively incumbent upon women. However, according to halakhah even two of these can also be performed by men. Nevertheless, *hadlik ner* (lighting of the Sabbath candles) and *challah* (taking of the dough) have by way of tradition come to be interpreted as 'women's mitzvot' (Kaufman 1995: 212). These two mitzvot centre on the celebration of the weekly Sabbath, and again take place in the private familial sphere. This is consistent with the gendered perception of women as bound to the home and the household, as opposed to men's more public role. The third of the women's mitzvot, *niddah* (menstruation or the menstruating woman), refers to what is generally called *taharat hamischpachah*, or the laws of family purity. Although these laws as such are incumbent upon all observant Jews, in practice they are the sole responsibility of the married woman, who must follow detailed prescriptions pertaining to her reproductive cycle and sexuality. This form of religious ritual in particular has received barely any, or very limited, attention in ethnographies of Hasidic communities, which take the male Jew as the central and normative person in the communities under study.

Once an Orthodox Jewish woman marries, every month she must start 'counting' from the onset of her menses, till seven days thereafter, a rule of conduct accompanied by detailed and halakhically prescribed vaginal self-inspection. During this period she is considered a niddah (menstruant), and therefore ritually impure (not to be confused with physical uncleanliness). Throughout this period, husband and wife must refrain from sexual contacts and any kind of direct or indirect 'inciting' behaviour, such as sharing the same bed, passing objects to each other, being seated next to each other, etc.[7] Breaking this law (even by an ignorant husband) is considered a grave transgression. After this period of checking and counting, the niddah must thoroughly cleanse herself (including the cutting of nails, removing any substances such as make-up, false teeth, contact lenses, etc.), before ritually immersing herself in the local *mikvah* (ritual bath), in order to regain a status of ritual purity. Only thereafter is she permitted (or encouraged) to resume sexual relations with her husband.

Identity and Belonging Among Newly Orthodox Jewish Women

One of the first widely known books to capture the public imagination on women's role in Hasidic communities dates from the 1980s, when journalist Lis Harris (1995, orig. 1985) published a personal account of her meetings with Lubavitcher Hasidim of New York, many of her conversations held with women within their own homes. The first researchers to address the problem of male bias in ethnographies of Hasidim and publish scholarly accounts of their own studies of Hasidic women as agents were probably Lynn Davidman (1991) and Debra R. Kaufman (1993, 1994, 1995). They both deal with ba'alot teshuvah in the U.S., women who have 'returned' or become 'newly Orthodox women' at some stage in their life.[9] With the traditionalist view of Judaism as an ethnically defined religious tradition, and conversion being difficult and somewhat rare, the Hasidic communities that originated in Eastern Europe generally do not practise any kind of 'missionary' activities, in contrast to many other contemporary religious traditionalist and fundamentalist movements. However, one particular Hasidic group, the Lubavitcher, also called Chabad, are both open to and actively recruit potential ba'alei teshuvah (masculine plural) and ba'alot teshuvah (feminine plural) – secular Jews who by personal choice become Orthodox Jews or 'return' to a strictly Orthodox Jewish lifestyle and community.

The phenomenon of returning to Orthodoxy increased significantly during the late 1960s and 1970s in the U.S., and then in Israel, where educational outreach programmes were formed (Kaufman 1993). Today, many Lubavitcher practise what some would almost call 'aggressive' proselytising campaigns. So-called mitzvah-mobiles drive around Jewish neighbourhoods or gatherings; the Lubavitch activists then persuade secular Jews to engage in small rituals such as helping men put on tefillin or offering women candlesticks for the lighting of Sabbath lights. The Lubavitcher have numerous educational institutions, programmes and residential houses (called Chabad) all over the world where returnees can be reeducated. Both their visibility and accessibility to outsiders is therefore higher than that of the other Hasidic and Misnagdic groupings. These can be called more isolationist types of communities (Manning 1999: 46, Stump 2000: 138). Not only do they to a great extent live separately from the surrounding society, but they are also uninterested in newcomers and outsiders, basically keeping to themselves. Before turning to my own study of strictly Orthodox Jewish women in such an isolationist community in Antwerp, I will briefly discuss what I interpret as central on the issue of gender and identity in studies of ba'alot teshuvah.

Methodologically, Davidman's (1991) and Kaufman's (1993, 1994, 1995) studies of newly Orthodox Jewish women and Bonnie Morris's (1995, 1998) historical study of Lubavitcher women of Crown Heights all employ some feminist epistemological premises for conducting research. They take women's experience and women's voices – as ethnographic informants or, in the case of Morris, as authors of written texts – as the starting point for conceptualising religious agency. These researchers move beyond the 'scholars' society' and the institutional public sphere as the centre of Orthodox tradition in which the male Hasid or strictly Orthodox Jew is taken as the primary agent of the religious life and the broader community. None of the authors go into detail on the way they appropriate feminist theories or methodologies in their research, although Kaufman (1995: 149–50) does claim to focus on 'these newly Orthodox Jewish women in their own voices and from their own perspectives. I focused on their everyday world "by taking it up from within," from the standpoint of them as "knowers actually and locally situated".' Morris's (1998) study of Lubavitcher women's activism, from the postwar period to the present, does not limit itself to newly Orthodox women, but is more a historical study of sources such as community archives, publications by the Lubavitcher Women's Organisation, etc. In opposition to Kaufman and Davidman, Morris thus focuses on strictly Orthodox women as involved in outreach programmes and as the proselytising agents themselves, rather than the 'converts' who are the subject of study for Davidman and Kaufman.

Despite their wholly different research populations among ba'alot teshuvah in the U.S.,[10] both Davidman and Kaufman situate their research questions against what they look upon as the fallacy of the secularisation thesis and the general rise of traditionalist religious movements. As feminist researchers, both tackle the apparent paradox of why assimilated Jewish women living in modern, liberal times in the U.S. would opt out of secular culture, bolstered by perceptions of deficient gender roles and ideology, and dominant liberal feminism within modern society. They question why these women choose to join a traditionalist religious community where women's role is defined by patriarchal ideology. Central to both studies is the process and the issue of conversion: women who have chosen (Kaufman) or are in the process of choosing (Davidman) to be taken on in a new community. Similarly, in both studies it appears that (at

least partly) the ba'alot teshuvah's choice is motivated by what seems to be a crisis or discontent with their individual gender identity, and by the need for a
communal identity in the sense of wanting to 'belong'.

According to Davidman (1991: 99), the women she studied who became
involved in a modern Orthodox synagogue, and the young secular Jewish
women who participated in a resocialisation programme at an institute of the
Lubavitch Hasidim, were clearly 'searching for an identity, for a clear definition
of who they were as people'. Noteworthy among the modern Orthodox Jewish
women was a rhetoric of individual choice, a view of 'the free construction of
the self', in explaining their return to Orthodoxy. As secularly raised, ethnic
Jews, both groups of ba'alot teshuvah were furthermore clearly in search of a
broader community of belonging, which was connected to their personal sense
of Jewishness and 'roots'. The women at the Lubavitcher residence had experienced personal familial or relational crises and also felt they 'had not been
given a strong sense of Jewish identity, be it ethnic or religious' (ibid.). Many of
these women had been searching and had tried other cults or fundamentalist
groups, but only felt complete after an individual quest for a sense of belonging in a community defined by a construction of ethnicity (Jewishness). This
was felt to be the expression of a core self, of roots, and perhaps a kind of
belonging at an imagined or even transcendental level of religion, spirituality
and continuity. Davidman (1991: 93) refers to the latter as 'being connected to
something larger than themselves', which some women described as their feeling during prayer services.

Beyond the need for communal identification, the ba'alot teshuvah in both
Davidman's and Kaufman's studies were clearly in search of a gender identity
that was distinctly feminine, tied to a clear-cut feminine gender role. At the personal level, these women had been disappointed and unhappy with the 'confusion' surrounding gender in modern secular liberal society. They were
particularly discontented with what they perceived to be the devaluation of values and structure in the private realm of the family. Both modern Orthodox and
Hasidic ba'alot teshuvah longed for a well-defined role of themselves as women,
wives and mothers and were deeply attracted by the conservative views pro-
vided by traditionalist religious discourse. Among these they championed the
arranged marriages among the Lubavitcher, and the religious values that were
placed on women's role within the nuclear family, which to them was wrongly
devalued in secular society. From Kaufman's interviews with already 'converted'
and established modern Orthodox and more traditionalist Orthodox ba'alot
teshuvah, including Hasidic women, similar identity politics became apparent.
These women had also been searching and had returned to their roots in an ethnically and transcendental-religiously defined community where they felt they
belonged. In terms of their personal gender identity, they had similarly felt dis-
illusioned with secular society's norms – or lack thereof – towards women, the
family and sexuality.

More than Davidman, Kaufman (1993) focuses on the way her informants
constructed gender, and the way they appropriated traditionalist patriarchal
religious gender ideology in order to redefine their identity as women. In their

eyes, the liberal feminist dominance of gender equality had eradicated the differences between women and men, to the detriment of certain feminine values
such as motherhood, nurturance and relationality. The laws surrounding niddah (the family purity laws), for example, were not seen as derogatory to
women, as they often are perceived outside of Orthodox Jewish communities.
Instead they interpreted the laws as 'giving structure, regulation, and control to
them over their sexuality' (Kaufman 1993: 9). Many women stressed the positive functions of the laws on sexual abstinence, such as an increase in mutual
attraction and sexual pleasure after the monthly period of separation. For others this period allowed them 'a bed of my own', and the right to privacy, con-
straining both women's and men's sexual desires. Almost all the women
Kaufman interviewed mentioned the laws of *onah*, the halakhic obligation on
men to satisfy their wives' sexual needs. The mitzvah of monthly ritual immersion in the mikvah was also interpreted in terms of a personal and communal
religious experience, transcending the self and spiritually 'connecting' to other
Jewish women in history.

The accommodation of and 'resistance' towards the patriarchal framework of
excluding women from the public realm of religion thus took place through
valorising and sacralising women's domestic and mothering role, their sexuality and bodies, and associating the 'female' or 'the feminine' with the spiritual
and the sacred as central to Orthodoxy (Kaufman 1994: 356): 'By accepting and
elaborating on the symbols and expectations associated with gender difference,
these ba'alot teshuvah claim they have some control over their sexuality and
marital lives.' So in these narratives of individual identity, gender sociality –
roles and activities to be performed as ordained by halakhah – was stressed as
well as culturality – religious symbolism and values. Kaufman suggests her
informants were even 'celebrating sexual difference', akin to a particular strand
of feminist thought. She compares her informants' views – who themselves
claim to be anti-liberal feminist in orientation - to what some writers have identified as contemporary 'radical feminists' or 'cultural radical feminists'. They
similarly argue for a celebration of women's culture and often harbour an essentialist gender ideology, stressing the unique biological, emotional, tempera-
mental, psychological and spiritual qualities of women. Certain radical
feminists also reject the liberal individualism of modern society, which they
identify as determined by patriarchal hegemonic values. Instead they wish to
revalorise the feminine and the possibility of 'women's culture', such as
women's connection to 'nature', the centrality of sexuality, procreation and
mothering. In this comparison of identity politics between ba'alot teshuvah
and certain cultural radical feminists, Kaufman does note one crucial difference. Although the Orthodox Jewish women in her study accommodate patriarchal gender ideology in view of their 'empowered' female identity
construction, they do not challenge the male hegemony in the public legal
community. However, they simply do not see Orthodox Judaism as a patriarchal
religion but claim it is 'feminine in principle'. Radical feminists, on the other
hand, reject all forms of patriarchal control and ideology and, as Kaufman

(1994: 359) argues, autonomously choose 'sex-segregation as a way of resisting male dominance and as a way of shaping society'.

Ba'alot teshuvah, on the other hand, merely capitalise on the sex-segregated social structure that is proscribed by patriarchal ideology in order to find satisfaction in their gender role and even their own women's culture. Not only do they sacralise and valorise the private, familial sphere, but this sphere becomes a world in itself, as it is expanded towards a broader 'homosocial world' of many shared activities with other women within the broader community (Kaufman 1993: 125). Through the relative segregation – especially among Hasidic women – from the broader society, and women's networks within the community through informal study groups, involvement in religious community activities, secular sisterhoods and voluntary work and charity events, this 'private' world of women to a great extent exists and functions separately from the men's 'public' world of religious (study and prayer) and secular (occupational) activity. Women and men in this respect can be seen as two clear, identifiable groups whose members are in face-to-face contact with each other, both with their own characteristics of sociality and culturality. The women in Kaufman's study clearly drew upon shared meanings and gender symbolism within this mode of social structure and practice, and their own – informal – modes of interaction. In my reading of Davidman's and Kaufman's studies of ba'alot teshuvah, and in comparison with my interviews with strictly Orthodox Jewish women, I detect some salient similarities and differences on the dimensions which determine the various levels of identity in relation to gender. The main differences, I suggest, are to a great extent influenced by the differing locations and subject positions taken up by the newly Orthodox women formerly discussed and those of my own research subjects who are 'frum-born' (Yiddish for 'pious') into an Orthodox Jewish community and way of life. In the following paragraph I shall provide a brief introduction to the strictly Orthodox Jewish communities of Antwerp, in order to situate where my research was carried out.

Antwerp: Last European Shtetl or the New Jerusalem?

The presence – and various immigration waves – of both Ashkenazi and later Sephardic Jews in the city of Antwerp can be dated as far back as the thirteenth century (Abicht 1988, 1994, Gutwirth 1968). The position of Antwerp as a transit centre for those travelling to the U.S. and as an important centre of the diamond industry even predates the Second World War. After the deportation and destruction of approximately half of Belgium's Jewish population by the Nazis in the Holocaust, some survivors returned, but it was mostly refugees, primarily from Eastern Europe, who settled in the city.[11] Among these were many Hasidic Jews from Poland, Hungary and Romania, among whom many were to participate in the recovery of the diamond industry. As for estimates of the postwar Jewish population of Antwerp, only Gutwirth's (1968, 1970) study of the Belzer Hasidim provides us with some numbers, estimating some 10,500 Antwerp Jews in 1966, approximately a quarter of the prewar population.

Although Hasidic and other Orthodox Jews most likely did live in Antwerp before the postwar immigration wave (Rabinowicz 1996: 39), the population probably showed a much greater diversity in terms of social, political and religious orientation than is the case today (Abicht 1988, Saerens 2000). A similar process of gradual hasidification can be assumed for Antwerp, can be ascertained for the postwar emigration of East European Jews to the U.S., notably resulting in a Jewish community that is for the greater part religiously observant, indeed Orthodox.

Of the estimated 15,000 to 18,000 Antwerp Jews today, the vast majority are affiliated with one of the two Orthodox religious congregations (Gutwirth 1999: 605). The Hasidic population is assumed to number some 5,000–6,000 inhabitants, which makes them approximately a third of the total – mostly Orthodox – population, indeed a unique situation compared to anywhere else in the world. The reconstitution of the predominantly Orthodox Antwerp Jewish community thus involved an evolution towards a relatively tight, cohesive community, located in a particular area of Antwerp, with its members acting upon the same structural networks of religious, economic, social and educational organisations: 'All of Jewish life in the town is hasidically coloured' (Gutwirth 1999: 605), thus giving Antwerp Jewry its unique character and sometimes the title of a contemporary shtetl.

Today there are three acknowledged Jewish religious congregations in Antwerp. The smallest is that of the small Sephardic community, the 'Congregation of the Portuguese Rite'.[12] Of the other two main religious congregations, the oldest is the Machsike Hadass, or the 'Orthodox Israeli Congregation', founded in 1892 and acknowledged by the state in 1910 (Bok 1986: 372). Machsike Hadass, which literally translates as 'strengtheners of the faith'[13] was from its inception explicitly traditionalist-oriented, initially non-Zionist, but according to Bok (ibid.) today does acknowledge the Jewish state of Israel. The present Hasidic communities of Antwerp are all affiliated with the Machsike Hadass, which gives this community its more rigorous or traditionalist character, compared to those who belong to the congregation of the Shomre Hadass ('defenders of the faith'). Although the leaders of the Shomre Hadass are very observant and traditionalist, the majority of its members are more lenient – many could be described as 'modern Orthodox' (Bok 1986: 372), or according to Abicht (1994: 136) 'conservative' Jewish. Affiliated with this congregation are also members who are more liberal or 'laxly' inclined. The majority of the Jews of Antwerp are members of one of these two Orthodox congregations, many of whom most likely identify as observant Jews – adherence to halakhah – are involved in the affiliated institutions and their networks, or at least have a strong Jewish identification. Particularly telling is Abicht's (1988: 64) claim that some 85 to 95 percent of Jewish children visit one of the various Jewish schools that exist in the city. Antwerp Jewry thus gains its unique character through the fact that whilst, relatively speaking, it may be small compared to, say, the number of Jews living in other cities (including other European cities such as London and Paris), it has a high degree of religious observance and social and geographical cohesion.

All three Jewish religious congregations are represented in the Central Consistory of the Israelites in Belgium in Brussels, which to date receives subsidies from the state for religious services. Both the Machsike Hadass and the Shomre Hadass have their own rabbinate, run different synagogues, supervise the *batai midrash* (houses of study), and regulate religious legal jurisdiction pertaining to internal, usually economical disputes (Gutwirth 1968). The congregations also provide all religious services to their members, supervising various butcheries and restaurants according to the dietary laws, and also the ritual circumcisers, mikvahs, etc. The congregations have formal and informal relations with numerous Jewish schools, some state subsidised (including a required secular curriculum) and other private religious schools, separate for boys and girls. The Machsike Hadass also functions as a coordinating and supervising structure for a variety of sub-congregations, including the Hasidic communities of Antwerp, who often have their own batai midrash and private religious schools (Rosenberg 2000). Hasidic Antwerp Jewry is also internally differentiated. The different Misnagdic or Hasidic groupings, for example, belong to even larger supranational communities or 'courts', whose members live spread out throughout the world. Hasidim from diverse courts are represented in Antwerp, including the Belzer (numerically the largest), the anti-Zionist Satmar, and many others such as the Vishnitz, Ger, Sandz, Chortkov, Lubavitch, Klausenberg, Barditchev and Bobov.[14]

Mothers of the Machsike Hadass

As part of the research for my PhD thesis, from the spring of 1998 through to autumn 1999, I conducted twenty-five in-depth interviews with self-identified Hasidic (from different groups such as the Belz, Satmar, Ger, etc.), 'Hasidic-oriented' and Misnagdic women, all living in Antwerp and affiliated with the Machsike Hadass congregation. Their ages ranged from thirty-eight to sixty-five years old and they self-identified from 'fairly involved' to the status of high-profile spokespersons within the community: as *rebbetsin* (wife of a rabbi) or involved in community activities, such as teaching, voluntary work or counselling.[15] Using the 'snowball' technique in locating informants, I did not gain access to one particular group, but was continuously referred to women from different Hasidic and non-Hasidic Orthodox backgrounds. They all turned out to know each other, refuting the suggestion that the different religious groups of Antwerp live in isolation from each other. Perhaps as a result of the specific situation of Orthodox Jewry in Antwerp – being a relatively small, yet cohesive community – the interaction between different traditionalist Jews, and especially the women, appeared to be quite high. Categorical distinctions were often rejected by my informants, some claiming 'we are not that different from each other', apart from, perhaps, details of dress and demeanour. Others refused to identify with any one group, stating they were 'open-minded', alternated between synagogues or were more or less 'Hasidic-oriented'.

The international character of Antwerp Orthodox Jewry was also corroborated by the diversity of the origins and places my informants had lived. Only four of the women I interviewed had actually been born and raised in the city of Antwerp itself. Although many parents and grandparents, or the women's husbands' ancestors, had come from Eastern Europe, consistent with their Hasidic or Misnagdic backgrounds, many of the women I interviewed were originally from the U.S., England, Israel, the Netherlands, etc. Although most of the women had been settled in Antwerp for some time, many had migrated more than once during their lives and were often married to men who similarly had international backgrounds. In other words, national identity was definitely diverse and not an issue for the women in this multilingual, diasporic traditionalist Orthodox Jewish community.

Although my traditionalist Jewish research population was diverse in terms of their precise religious identification, all the women I interviewed were 'frum-born', that is they came from or had been raised in religiously observant families. So although some women claimed to have intensified both their observance and their belief throughout their lives, - sometimes through marrying even more strictly Orthodox men than themselves - none had been raised or came from a secular family or upbringing, to 'convert' at some stage in their lives, like the ba'alot teshuvah studied by Kaufman, Davidman and Morris. These wholly different backgrounds from the ba'alot teshuvah in the studies by Kaufman and Davidman, I suggest, may be accountable for some notable differences in the way these women discursively constructed their identities.

Gender Identity Among the 'Frum-born': Quality as Difference through Sociality and Practice

From the theoretical perspective of gender as a culturally constructed category, as advanced in the Introduction, I set out in my interviews to elicit how my respondents understood or were positioned regarding the differences between women and men. All my interviewees unanimously agreed that men and women were different, created differently by God, having different obligations and responsibilities according to halakhah, yet by no means could one be conceived of as inferior or superior to the other. The difference between women and men was taken to be obvious – and my questions therefore often interpreted as somewhat nonsensical – and in the first place founded on an implicit ideology of naturalised, essential sexual difference, as common in many, particularly Mediterranean, cultures (Bourdieu 2001). When I probed further, the differences between women and men were differentially legitimated and explained through a multiplicity of discourses, besides merely 'religion'. Initially, however, the context for the understanding of gender in terms of sexual difference was nearly always referred to as the institution of marriage, as the expression of 'complementarity' or 'harmony', ultimately founded as the divine commandment of marriage, and procreation as God's purpose for the creation of 'two halves becoming one whole'.

Secondly, a sine qua non that informed everything I read and researched on the position of women in Orthodox Judaism was the tenet of women and men as 'different but of equal value'. According to the literature and my research subjects, this premise could not be emphasised enough in any discussion of religion – what Orthodox Jewish scholar Michael Kaufman (1995: 58) calls theological equality – and daily life. All my informants agreed that although women and men were viewed as different in their community and religious tradition, they are equal to each other in worth; no one is intrinsically superior or inferior to the other. Beyond these first hegemonic religious discourses of sexual difference for marriage and procreation, and equal value regardless of difference, various other types of discourse are present in the literature by Orthodox Jewish writers and were applied by my own informants in order to account for the differences between women and men.

In his introduction to *The Woman in Jewish Law and Tradition*, for example, Orthodox Jewish scholar Michael Kaufman (1995) uses both religious and scientific rhetoric in order to provide legitimation for the distinctive gender spheres in Judaism. Kaufman (1995: xxix) sees the differences between men and women as 'innate' and 'noninterchangeable' within an essentialist framework that conflates sex and gender. This ideology of sexual difference as gender difference serves to support the author's rejection of feminism (or what he calls masculofeminism) that unjustly glorifies the man's public role in Judaism, opposed to women's devalued role within the private sphere of the home. Kaufman critiques these masculofeminists for their view on gender differences as culturally determined, as if the new-born infant were a *tabula rasa* upon which society and rearing practices can inscribe anything, including masculinity and femininity. The author then reverts to scientific 'evidence' which supports his idea of sexual difference. He first claims that recent studies in the 'physical and behavioural sciences have substantiated the thesis of a predominantly biological basis for sexually differentiated behaviour in humans' (xxx–xxxi). Furthermore, he says that evidence from 'genetics, brain research, sociology and psychology confirm that the primary determinant of sexually differentiated behaviour is biology and not culture', referring to, for example, Carol Gilligan's (1982, 1997) famous research on women and moral development.

Kaufman's discourse in attributing essential characteristics in terms of sexual/gender difference to women and men thus functions as a justification for commitment to halakhah and traditionalist gender prescriptions, in spite of the changes in women's role in modern society. Opposed to the 'masculofeminist' version of feminism which aspires for the equality of men and women based on patriarchal values, Kaufman claims the essential differences between women and men do not necessarily coincide with women's subordination, but can be exalted within the framework of Jewish tradition. Distinct gender roles and the valorisation of essential feminine virtues, attributes and institutions thereby appear to be in accordance with the high legal status of women in halakhah and the importance of the family. Notwithstanding a woman's exemption from paradigmatic public religious rituals, she can still lead a 'full' religious life. Thus, according to Kaufman (1995: 25), a woman's inherent qualities, such as her 'sensitivity, perception, gentleness and flexibility', are suited to her role within the family and private sphere. As such, they are in contrast with men, whose proclivity is to the public domain and whose 'abstract and analytical mentality [is] weaker in these spheres…'

In other more personal accounts by Orthodox Jewish women themselves, the same type of rhetoric that sets out to valorise women's unique spiritual, biological and psychological attributes, rituals and imagery, even to the extent of a celebration of the ideology of sexual difference, is to be found. Tamar Frankiel (1990), for example, a lecturer in comparative religion and convert to Judaism, in her book on the position of women in traditional Judaism, attempts to reconcile feminism with a traditional Orthodox Jewish way of life. Throughout the book Frankiel points to the special qualities of women, such as their intuition, their 'capacities for relationship and involvement' (46–47), and other feminine abilities that warrant their prescribed role in Jewish religious practice. Frankiel (1990: 109) furthermore claims that women actually enjoy a different kind of spirituality from that of men: 'a strongly relational orientation prevails, giving feminine spirituality a definite communal and moral ethical bent from the beginning.' Similar to Michael Kaufman (1995) and as an academic observant Orthodox Jewish woman, Frankiel seeks to legitimise gender roles according to halakhah through a discourse of sexual difference in terms of psychology and morality. Both authors make their arguments in a location, or in the context of – and opposed to – Western modern liberal and predominantly secular society where gender equality has become the ideological norm.

In Davidman's (1991) study of both modern Orthodox and Hasidic Lubavitch ba'alot teshuvah, the women she interviewed similarly often reverted to essentialist understandings of women's nature. Whilst the rabbis in the modern Orthodox community seemed to mix traditionalist views on women's roles in the home with more modern views on egalitarian gender roles, in the teachings in the Hasidic classes Davidman participated in, women's role in childbearing and nurture was seen as 'a metaphor for her essential nature' (166). The process of resocialising these modern women towards Orthodoxy required a 'radical reconceptualisation of femininity', including the idea that 'women's nature is rooted in their biology and expressed in all aspects of their beings'. A similar profamilial stance, according to Kaufman's (1993) study of established ba'alot teshuvah, accompanied a view of women as essentially inclined to harbour values associated with care, nurturance and interconnected relationships. As with the tendencies in Frankiel's (1990) account to delineate specific feminine forms of spirituality, Davidman's research also points to a strong celebration of sexual difference amongst ba'alot teshuvah, often to the extent of imbuing the sacred itself with feminine attributes, or the assertion that women may innately possess certain spiritual abilities which are superior to those of men.

In contrast to both the literature by Orthodox Jewish scholars mentioned above, and the research on ba'alot teshuvah, the Hasidic, Hasidic-oriented and Misnagdic women of Antwerp I interviewed did not all revert to religious discourse in order to explain the essential innate differences between women and men. My general impression was that the more Hasidic the women I interviewed, the more likely they were to draw on essentialist constructions of gender and the more apt they were to explain these in religious terms. For example, the obligation for men to study Talmud would be explained by their 'natural attraction' towards logical or analytical thinking, as opposed to women, who were more in tune with their feelings, being sensitive, intuitive and having more relational capacities. The differences were then explained in religious terms as in 'God created women and men that way', and these abilities concurred with their proper roles and perhaps their spiritual make-up. However, not everyone did rely on religious notions of gender difference as in behaviour and personality traits between women and men. Others maintained the differences between women and men were more psychological and social, following their roles rather than embedded in their biology. Some even denied there were any absolute differences that could be ascribed to religious philosophy. Here, the gender discourse these women applied was clearly borrowed from a multiplicity of ideological frameworks, beyond religion, such as popular psychology and medicine, magazines, 'common sense knowledge', or personal viewpoints inferred from experience. Hence, I doubt that these women's viewpoints would differ dramatically from those of many secular women in the same age category.

Thus my informants, who were all frum-born – although some of them may gradually have become more Hasidic during their lives – appeared to be less essentialist in accounting for gender than is evident in the research by Kaufman (1993) and Davidman (1991) on North American ba'alot teshuvah, and even in the literature by Orthodox Jewish writers themselves such as Michael Kaufman (1995), Frankiel (1990) or another known 'Orthodox feminist' Blu Greenberg (1998). The ba'alot teshuvah had not only been reeducated into religious philosophy and observance, but their reasons for consciously returning to a religious life and community had often been precisely motivated by their attraction to traditionalist gender ideology. This difference, I suspect, explains to some extent the fact that many of my informants were less cognisant of or, better put, less interested in religious discourse on gender. For them, difference was more self-evident, something they did not need to question or justify. Often, when I tried to probe further about women's spirituality, many women answered that they were not exactly sure, or this was a subject their rabbi-husband would know more about. As for the literature on women's role in contemporary Orthodox Judaism by authors such as Tamar Frankiel and Blu Greenberg, both hare the same overt interest in religious discourse on gender and gender ideology as the ba'alot teshuvah. For from the position of a personal quest these women have similarly been confronted with the issue of feminism – understood in the form of liberal equality – and gender roles in secular modern society. Even more so, these authors have studied Jewish religions gender ideology and often – selectively – scientific material themselves in order to (albeit to different degrees) to be able to ground and defend traditionalist views on women and men.

So, in a way, my interviewees replicated a two sexes/two genders model, for besides the 'fact' of sexual difference, gender itself was not essentialised into any one kind of discursive formation (religious, psychological, subjective), at least not to the extent one might expect to be the case in such a traditionalist community. In terms of identity, for the frum-born women of the Machsike Hadass, individual gender identity was much less pronounced than among the ba'alot teshuvah, or Orthodox writers actively confronting and reflecting upon gender in the context of modernity as such. Although the degrees of essentialism differed between the more modern Orthodox and the Hasidic returnees in both Kaufman's and Davidman's studies, and the factors driving these women to join such gender-conservative communities were in no means uniform, gender functioned as a highly important dimension within the interviews. For the frum-born women of the Machsike Hadass, by contrast, gender as an issue appears to be much less relevant in their self-definition throughout the interviews. Additionally, their gender discourse was often even nonessentialist, although in practice, dualism in terms of gender roles and (religious) obligations was paramount. In relation to the model of identity proposed by Pinxten and Verstraete, for my strictly Orthodox Jewish interviewees, therefore, gender appeared evident at the level of *sociality* rather than explicitly relevant in terms of *culturality*, which seemed to be the case for the ba'alot teshuvah in Kaufman and Davidman's studies.

This became especially evident in comparison with the way the ba'alot teshuvah in Kaufman's study reverted to religion in their celebration of the female and in invoking feminine symbolic imagery. Many of the women in Kaufman's study elaborated on their important role as women in Jewish symbolism, mythology and ritual, for instance by referring to the Sabbath as feminine, or the *Shekinah*, the indwelling of God, as feminine. In Kaufman's (1993: 53) words: 'The selected bits and pieces of tradition and theology they chose to relate strongly suggest that they consciously reformulate that orthodoxy in their own image. They associate the sacred and themselves with positive purpose and positive self-definition. This ideology is held in place through the structure of their everyday lives'. Many of the Hasidic interviewees even went so far as to claim that women may be more spiritually inclined, closer to God and in some ways superior to men. In this context they asserted that God told Moses to teach the Torah first to the women and afterward to men, or that the reason why women were exempt from time-bound commandments was that they were by nature more spiritually inclined. According to Kaufman, the contrast with the non-Hasidic women she interviewed can be explained by the fact that Hasidism incorporates mystical and cabalistic thought, and her interviewees had capitalised on feminine principles that exist within Jewish mysticism such as the importance of *binah* or wisdom, which is referred to as feminine or the Shekinah.

By contrast, even the most Hasidic among the frum-born women I interviewed in Antwerp did not revert to any such feminine principles when I probed them on their understanding of spirituality. Even though the vast majority of the women I interviewed were educated, often intellectuals, and many were themselves teachers or retired teachers of subjects such as Hebrew or religious philosophy, they did not particularly emphasise any of the gender-related symbolism which appeared so relevant for the ba'alot teshuvah. Likewise, my informants were much less forthcoming on the topic of sexuality compared to Kaufman's research subjects, a point which Kaufman (1993: 78) herself raises as a possible difference between returnees and the frum-born. No references whatsoever were made to the mitzvah of onah for men, the commandment to satisfy their wives sexually. Whereas some women were prepared to discuss the laws of family purity, they did not in the least draw on personal experience, but stressed the importance of the laws in general terms. One Misnagdic woman, who used to give bridal education to girls who were engaged to be married, told me how in her classes she tried to transfer a positive attitude to her students concerning the laws of niddah. This applied especially to the ritual of immersion, not only by explaining the practical 'benefits', but also the symbolism surrounding the rituals, with metaphors such as rebirth, the mikvah as the womb, etc. However, as was also repeated by other informants, regardless of the meanings one could attach to such rituals – whether symbolic or practical – or however sexual abstinence, checking and ritual immersion were experienced individually, all these forms of legitimation or explanation remained subservient to the mitzvah of niddah itself. This was first and foremost perceived as an obligatory commandment and practice that was divinely ordained, and therefore in theory did not require any further justification.

As a religious tradition of orthopraxis rather than orthodoxy, it may come as no surprise that gender is prominent for the dimension of sociality in strictly Orthodox Jewish communities. While the centrality of practising religion by abiding by religious law is characteristic for both the ba'alot teshuvah and the frum-born women, in the subject positions taken by the latter in my interviews, gender was definitely explained in terms of proper roles for women and men, thus emphasising sociality above culturality. Although the gender constructions pertaining to the essential differences between women and men varied, both the 'fact' of sexual difference itself and the tenet of 'different yet of equal value' were understood as ultimately always connected to women's childbearing capacity. Woman's role in raising the children and therefore being bound to the home was seen as obvious and evident in universal terms. Those women I interviewed who did – and those who did not – use essentialist discourse on gender were equally adamant on the centrality of the different religious obligations for women and men in any discussion of gender. Many women even answered my questions on whether women had any innate abilities or characteristics which explained their differences in Orthodox Jewish religious traditions and communities, in terms of women's different religious obligations – their mitzvot – thus what women and men *did* differently rather than what made them essentially different. Man's intellect and brain was seen as more attuned to his fundamental religious obligation, which is to study Torah, and 'logical, objective thinking' for the performance of Talmud study. Women, on the other hand, as mothers and keepers of the home, needed such qualities as 'feeling' and 'softness' for their proper role for instilling and continuing tradition.

With this last remark on strictly Orthodox Jewish women's private yet particular role as a mother and religious educator within the home, I move to the second main argument of this paper, which illustrates the multifaceted relationship between gender and identity. From the interviews with the women of the Machsike Hadass it became clear that gender appeared to be more a question of sociality than culturality. In the self-definition of individual identity, gender was simply less relevant than ethnic/religious identification, compared with the studies of newly Orthodox women. In the next section, I argue that at the level of group identity, and also the community – as is the case for many other religious traditionalist, fundamentalist and nationalist contexts – gender appears to function as an important structuring principle. This point is again illustrated with some of the statements made by the women of the Machsike Hadass, and further supported by some recent feminist thinking on fundamentalist identity politics on a global scale.

Community Identities in Conflict: Strictly Orthodox Jewish Women as 'Bearers of the Collective'

When accounting for the strong anti-feminist rhetoric by Lubavitcher women activists, – next to their promotion of positive models of female spirituality and family life – Bonnie Morris (1995) points to the priority given to ethnic survival and the association of both women's subordinate status and the consecutive feminist movement within the Christian or secularised majority culture. Apart from the clear insistence on maintaining traditional gender ideology and roles as a part of simply upholding tradition, other factors certainly play a role in the way strictly Orthodox Jewish authorities and communities perceive feminism and the demand for gender equality as a 'threat'. The feminist movement and its critiques of patriarchal religions was not only often seen as anti-Semitic; it was also felt to be a threat to the family, to women's role in reproduction and as mother and educator of the young. As an 'ethnically' defined religious tradition, and especially one in which according to halakhah Jewish identity is transferred only by the mother onto the child, the modern demand for the autonomy and equality of women was seen as a possible threat not only to the survival of religious tradition, but also to ethnic continuity. Particularly since the Holocaust and the great rate of assimilation amongst Jews, survival has been proclaimed a crucial issue by Hasidic and other strictly Orthodox authorities, and was emphasised by a number of the women I spoke to. The invocation of the religious commandment of procreation, and the prohibition of – or at least restrictions on – birth control that are propagated by religious authorities, ensure that women in strictly Orthodox Jewish communities are seen as 'the biological producers of children/people', and therefore quite literally attributed the status of 'bearers of the collective' (Yuval-Davis 1997).

Beyond the specific characteristics of the definition of ethnic identity in racial terms, and its current usage within the particular historical context of the growth of strictly Orthodox Jewry, the broader cultural notion of women as 'bearers of the collective' recurs in various contemporary religious traditionalist, fundamentalist and nationalist movements throughout the world, as argued by feminist scholars such as Sahgal and Yuval-Davis (1992a), Yuval-Davis (1997), and illustrated in various cross-cultural collections (e.g., Charles and Hintjens 1998, Howland 1999, Moghadam 1994a, Sahgal and Yuval-Davis

1992b). First, however, the question whether the frum-born Jewish women from the strictly Orthodox Antwerp community I interviewed may be straight-forwardly considered 'fundamentalists' needs to be touched upon briefly.

Jewish Fundamentalisms

In most of the general ethnographical studies of contemporary Hasidim spoken of earlier (e.g., Heilman 1992, Kranzler 1995, Mintz 1994), the concept of fun-damentalism in order to describe these traditionalist religious communities is, somewhat curiously, seldom used.[17] Webber (1987: 97) is critical of the pejo-rative and outsider concept of fundamentalism as applicable to contemporary traditionalist Jewish identities, and prefers to take a closer look at the ideolog-ical structures and circumstances that have given rise to the usage of this term: 'whether it be seen as a "response" to modernism or simply as a re-statement of traditional orthodox tenets which modernists classify as "fundamentalist" so as to make sense of their position appear normative by contrast.' On the other hand, in the publications on fundamentalism ever since Marty and Appleby's prestigious Fundamentalism Project, and as unambiguously becomes clear in Heilman and Friedman's (1991) contribution to the first volume of their series, the contemporary haredim of Israel are clearly identified as Jewish fundamen-talists. Moreover, the authors consider the haredi as the successors of the his-torical Hasidic movement, an early form of Jewish religious fundamentalism. Other authors similarly consider the traditionalist movement of Hasidism orig-inating in the seventeenth and eighteenth century as the 'roots' of Jewish fun-damentalism today (Armstrong 2000, Stump 2000). Despite the obvious complexities in applying fundamentalism as an overarching concept for what is identified as a world-wide growing phenomenon, many scholars – however critically or thoughtfully – taking a comparative rather than a strictly ethno-graphical viewpoint, refer to the contemporary haredim as one of the two main forms of Jewish fundamentalism, the other being religious Zionism, predomi-nantly embodied in Gush Emunim (the Block of the Faithful).

Whilst Gush Emunim oppose secular Zionism, the vision of many Israeli haredim on the erection – and territorial expansion or repossession – of a reli-gious state does not necessarily share what is often seen to be one of religious fundamentalism's defining features: the refutation of the separation between religion and politics, between the 'church and the state'. Even though they do believe in the coming of the Messiah, the Satmar Hasidim, for example, are adamant in their condemnation of the religious Zionist literal vision of the Land of Israel as the context for the Messiah's arrival. For this reason, a writer like Lustick (1993) rejects the application of the term fundamentalism for the majority of any haredi (Hasidic or Misnagdic) communities, for they do not politicise their messianism in the sense that they are seeking to transform soci-ety through state politics. Nonetheless, in practice they may be politically active in the securing and preservation of their own 'isolationist' communities. Other authors see these differences in terms of degrees, categorising the religious Zionists as the more active or innovative radical type, opposed to the more qui-escent or conservative haredi (Cromer 1993, Friedman 1993, Hyman 1999).

So even if many haredim do not ascribe to a conflation between the national and the religious in the definition of their collective identity, and Gush Emunim may be held to be the 'paradigmatic' form of Jewish religious fundamentalism, most authors appear to agree on the overwhelming similarities between haredim and other forms of what is mostly identified as religious fundamentalism. The differential categorisation on grounds of Zionism, non-Zionism or anti-Zionistic perspectives can moreover be de-emphasised by broadening the definition of 'politics' to more than just party politics and state control. Most haredi in Israel in fact are politically active, and often do appeal to the state in order to support their own political and economic projects (Yuval-Davis 1999). Both groups are furthermore extremely politically motivated in that they reject secularism tout court, in that all spheres of life, including the personal, are seen to be regulated by halakhah, religious law.

When the focus is shifted to strictly Orthodox Jewish communities in the diaspora, categorisations become complicated even further. Within the context of secular states with freedom of religion, such as in the U.S. and Europe, these communities do not share the same political struggles vis-à-vis their governments, but can take their isolationism even further. Thus, strictly Orthodox Jews can have a national identity that is that of a U.S. citizen, Belgian, British, etc. For the individual, Jewish ethnic/religious identification nevertheless remains paramount, as was also claimed by many of my own interviewees. The grounds for comparison are further supported by the increasing internationalisation of strictly Orthodox Jewry (see above for Antwerp), and if not an overt orientation towards Israel, at least a positioning vis-à-vis Israel lives in the consciousness of many diasporic strictly Orthodox Jews. In any case, in general, all strictly Orthodox Jews aim to 'sacralise the profane' in their daily lives. Indeed, for these traditionalists, religious identity circumscribes everyday life and experience. As one of the women I interviewed said to me: 'We live and breathe religion; it is not limited to the way you celebrate Christmas once a year.'

Gendered Boundaries

Taking into account the same reservations and stressing the necessity for continuous contextualisation and specification of the community or movement under study, I nonetheless believe that the discourse on religious identity and tradition reproduced by the women I interviewed did show many of the same structural features that have been noted for the gender identity politics of many contemporary movements and collectivities that are referred to as 'fundamentalist'. The securing of identity vis-à-vis that of the 'other' – usually seen as 'modern', 'Western', 'secular' – who is perceived as a threat through clearly defined boundaries is one of these main characteristics. Although the context for the rise of fundamentalist movements and the contemporary 'crisis of identities' in general has been referred to as that of 'modernity and its discontents', the relationship with modernity is also often described as ambiguous or 'dialectic' (Silberstein 1993: 6). For the growth of these communities has clearly depended on and is known for appropriating precisely typical 'modern' elements in order to thrive, in particular technology, the media, etc. Whatever important differences may exist between and within different kinds of religious fundamentalisms, the battle to preserve what is understood to be the traditional religious identity of the community, almost cross-culturally involves opposing one feature of Western modernity. This concerns gender equality and in particular the disintegration of patriarchal society as a major historical development throughout the West and beyond during the twentieth century. In this 'control of women' through, for instance, strict gender segregation or preventing women's access to the public domain and positions of (religious) authority, religious discourse is then often invoked as a means of justification. This invariably takes place in an essentialist mode, such as in the name of 'timeless tradition', defying the internal and cross-cultural dynamics of gender throughout time.

As was argued in a previous paragraph, for many of the strictly Orthodox Jewish women in my case study there seemed to be a tension between continuity and innovation of traditional gender patterns, with gender appearing as a pattern of generational sociality and practice, rather than overt, explicit, essentialist gender ideology in accounting for clear-cut gender roles. Typical of traditionalist Judaism in general, the preservation of religious identity is expressed through halakhic observance – thus in the realm of behaviour rather than, or at least above, religious doctrine and belief. Beyond individual identity, the regulation of women's behaviour is nonetheless crucial in the definition and reproduction of both the identity of the group and the 'imagined' community. Gender functions not only as a marker of difference between women and men, but as a marker for the difference between the group's identity versus the 'other', in this case secular modern society, or, as my informants referred to it, 'the outside world'. Beyond the construction of women as the 'biological reproducers' of strictly Orthodox Jewish ethnicity, and as the primary agents of socialisation of the young (Moghadam 1994b: 18), women also function as the 'symbolic border guards and as embodiments of the collectivity, whilst at the same time being its cultural reproducers' (Yuval-Davis 1997: 23), or the 'cultural carriers' of group identity (Saghal and Yuval-Davis 1992a: 8).

The 'burden of reproduction and representation' means women and their 'proper' behaviour in many fundamentalist, nationalist and ethnic projects often symbolise the integrity or 'honour' and the boundaries of the collective identity. The control of women's sexuality and their bodily praxis, as in restrictions on ways to comport oneself, dress and behave, appear to be characteristic of many patriarchal societies, cultures and religious traditions. Yet in those contemporary communities which are seeking to preserve and reproduce 'tradition', this control is often not only intensified, but takes centre stage in maintaining the difference between the own and the other's identity. In the case of strictly Orthodox Jewry, and as testified in many of my interviews, gender functions as a marker for further difference and isolationism. However, from the 'native viewpoint' change is attributed to the other and therefore an external cause is identified for any increase of gender conservatism.

According to many of my interviewees *tzniut* or modesty was one, if not the most important principle circumscribing women's religiosity. Besides the mitzvot (the ritual and ethical obligations and injunctions that were seen as gender neutral and thus equally incumbent on women and men) women as keepers of the home and the private world were to follow an ethic of modesty, in concordance with men's specific public ritual role. This covers a broad arena of physical appearance and demeanour, yet also speech, thought, and activities which in general are seen as related to a woman's place in the private sphere. These make sure she remains bound to this sphere and its 'inside activities', for 'the honour of the daughter of the king is indoors', as was quoted to me on numerous occasions.

Parallel to what outsiders perceive as details of difference in the dress of strictly Orthodox Jewish men from different Hasidic and non-Hasidic communities (e.g., jacket, side-locks), the precise clothing requirements of women, such as colours, hats, and colours and types of stockings, vary from one religious authority to another and are determined by custom. All the strictly Orthodox Jewish women I interviewed kept to the basic rules of tzniut. They wore a wig or kerchief, avoided 'ostentatious' clothing, such as bright colours or high heels, covered knees and elbows and décolleté, yet were also obliged to wear distinctly 'feminine' modest clothing. My informants were keen to emphasise that tzniut referred to much more than looks, although the extent and areas to which it reached was difficult for some to explain. Tzniut also meant to behave appropriately: not to shout, sing, or laugh out loud. 'Inner modesty' was described as not 'to be arrogant or proud', 'to be rough', or 'display your wealth or your wisdom' and tzniut even determined the things you would read or talk about. When probing for the reasons behind tzniut, the main rationale put forward was that the body of a woman was beautiful and had to be treated with dignity and respect. The woman must be modest in order not to 'provoke other men' or 'put the wrong thoughts into their minds' or 'cause them to be led into temptation'. Covering the body also meant not to expose or 'cheapen it outside' and to 'keep it beautiful and only for the husband'. Through behaving and dressing modestly, these women also felt they could control their husband's sexuality and their faithfulness to them.

The regulation of women's sexuality as an essential tool for the construction of collective identity is also expressed in the laws and rituals surrounding niddah or the family purity laws, which were discussed earlier. The individual responsibility of each woman to abide by these laws was interpreted by my informants as of utmost relevance, not only for the husband and family, but for the community, or, as one Hasidic woman who was originally from Israel literally said to me, 'for the sake of the nation'. Research on contemporary religious Zionist discourse on the laws of niddah in Israel in particular shows how the meaning of niddah has expanded to the public domain, rhetorically linking the importance of the practice of the laws by women to collective Jewish identity (Yanay and Rapoport 1997). In an analysis of literature by Orthodox Jewish women from various backgrounds, Myers and Litman (1995) suggest the discourse on the traditional role of observant women, including the practice of the family purity laws, is more apologetic when written by the women who were formerly secular or who are trying to reach a secular audience, in that they require a 'counter-ideology', incorporating concepts and symbols from the secular world in order to justify Orthodox practice. The literature by frum-born women, the authors argue, is not in need of the same level of sophistication in explaining the laws women must follow, as obedience to God and the fact that the laws have been practised for generations in itself suffice. Despite the precedence of sociality – the often nonessentialist understandings of gender and the absence of an ideology of female superiority – rather than cultural or symbolic meanings in explaining and accounting for the laws of family purity among the frum-born women in my interviews, similar rhetoric was used in attributing collective responsibilities to women. This was expressed in their correct individual behaviour, which will guarantee the 'purity' and the 'modesty' of the whole community. It therefore seems to be the case that women and their behaviour functions as an important symbol in diverse strictly Orthodox communities, and in similar ways in various identity politics in many religious traditionalist, fundamentalist or nationalist movements.

As frum-born traditionalists, however, from their own perspective and in their own voice, many of my interviewees denied that they were doing anything fundamentally different to what their mothers or grandmothers had done, although some did admit to a possible increase in gender conservatism in recent times. Interestingly they attributed this to the 'outside world', which for them used to be 'decent', yet had evolved into a society of 'unisex', with too much 'freedom' and where 'everything is possible and everything is allowed', and in general moral decline. From the native viewpoint, paradoxically, change was necessary in order to remain the same. Although many of my middle-aged informants had been brought up in a society in which everyone was 'decent' – women still wore skirts and sexuality was not made public and for sale – their sons and daughters needed much more protection, so that they would not be exposed to the dangers of modern society and possibly 'glitch'. In practice this had meant an increase in both isolationism and gender conservatism, the latter especially consequential for girls and women, who must keep bound to the home and private world. So even though the gender ideologies put forward by my interviewees were by no means always or completely essentialist, an increase in gender conservatism, as in more gender segregation at younger ages, a more stringent application of modesty laws (such as applying the rules of dress at a younger age than was even halakhically prescribed), was deemed necessary due to what my interviewees strongly disapproved of as the decline in sexual morals and the dominant dangerous gender ideology in the surrounding society.

The principle of tzniut or modesty in itself was linked to the broader context of a woman's place within the family or private sphere, and keeping her bound to her family and obligations so as not to be attracted by the 'outside world'. However, this was definitely not interpreted as submissive confinement. As all my informants made clear, women's religious duties certainly did not mean that she could not study, work, fulfil herself, or even take positions of authority or responsibility. There were no religious objections to a woman, for instance, becoming the director of a big company. In practice, however, and which is especially the case in diasporic and smaller communities outside of

Israel within secular societies such as Antwerp, the rules of modesty simply make it impossible for strictly Orthodox Jewish girls and women to pursue studies or apply for many jobs, as mixed environments are out of the question. Many a young woman had had to give up a job among *goyim* because of the 'dirty jokes' or the general atmosphere which she did not feel comfortable with. As for education, many of the young strictly Orthodox Jewish men go off to yeshivas abroad, and some young women will visit special Jewish women's colleges – usually for teacher training courses – in Israel or other cities of the diaspora. For most strictly Orthodox Jewish women, however, university for example is simply out of the question, although in theory there is no reason why they could not study or obtain a degree. Many of my informants in fact had studied later on in life; one woman even solved the problem of a course in alternative medicine she could not follow because of the presence of male students, by inviting the teacher to her own home, with a number of other secular women eventually joining in the lessons. Another woman told me that perhaps new possibilities would open up with information technology and virtual communication, where the difficulties of the physical, mixed-gender, public secular world would be overcome. In spite of the possibilities for the strictly Orthodox Jewish women I interviewed to educate themselves, their interest in secular culture and literature – within the boundaries of what they considered to be decent and nonvulgar – travel, work, etc. and individual self-fulfilment in general remained subservient to their most important duty of maintaining the home. Through their religious obligations as mothers and in their domestic role they saw themselves as of utmost importance in the maintenance of stability, tradition and religion as such, or as central to the reproduction of the community's identity. Thus in relation to (and mapped onto) the model of identity set forth by Pinxten and Verstraete, gender functions in terms of meaning and culturality at the level of the identity construction of the community vis-à-vis that of the 'other' (nontraditionalist or 'modern', secular, individualist, etc.). Within the boundaries of the community, this particular configuration of gender accompanies concrete patterns of sociality (practices of gender or processes of engendering in terms of learning, roles, behaviour, institutional and spatial arrangements) for concrete groups of women (and men).

Conclusion

In the introduction to this essay I briefly presented some theoretical excursions on gender and identity, selected from a multitude of possible viewpoints, frameworks and genealogies within the field of feminist scholarship. Although the concepts of gender and identity in their basic meanings of 'difference' and 'sameness' are at once central to, yet highly complex and polysemic, in feminist research, most current scholars believe both notions and their mutual relationship should be conceived of as dynamic and nonessentialist. This approach is in accordance with the basic perspective of identity that underlies this volume. Beyond the conceptual difficulties, I have also pointed to the fact that, from a feminist perspective, both notions are invested with political meanings, which is continuously illustrated throughout the remains of this chapter.

The main purpose of this essay was to show how by focusing on one particular case, gender can be viewed as both determined by sociality and culturality, and can be seen as more than just an individual 'attribute'. As an analytical category it can prove to be important and often even central to the construction of collective identity. Drawing on my own analysis of the position of women in strictly Orthodox Jewish communities, I made two main arguments. First a comparison was made between existing research on newly Orthodox Jewish women in the U.S. and an analysis of my own interviews with 'frum-born' strictly Orthodox Jewish women affiliated with the Machsike Hadass congregation of Antwerp in Belgium. The comparison shows several differences between the two research populations in terms of individual identity. Whilst for the first the rhetoric of choice, essentialism and ideologies of female superiority, in short the cultural dimension, appeared important, for the frum-born women, gender was more a question of sociality. Akin to analytical concepts such as material/symbolic, discourse/practice, objective/subjective (Bourdieu 2001), both sociality and culturality are used as analytical and relative concepts, as stated in the introduction to this volume. Similarly, in relation to the determination of gender, and depending on the context, in reality both dimensions are held to be at work simultaneously. The comparison revealed an additional point of difference: for the frum-born women in my case study, ethnic-religious individual identification turned out to be more relevant than gender identity. Obviously there were and will always be important differences between individual women, as there are between the subcommunities and communities themselves. As I have suggested on a number of occasions throughout this essay, categorisations carry many risks, and broader contexts – e.g., Israel versus diasporic communities – and other forms of location besides gender, religion, ethnicity are fundamental in situating viewpoints, whether they belong to ethnographic informants or the interpreters themselves. Although I have not gone into detail about any of the methodological frameworks and considerations in both the research dealt with or my own, the idea of 'subject positions' as briefly outlined in the Introduction and the general notion of locations or 'situated knowledges' (Haraway 1988) in feminist research have guided my interpretations throughout.

In the second part of the essay I shifted my focus from women as 'agents' of religious practice to women as 'symbols' (Sered 1999) of religious discourse, to make way for a more feminist critical discussion of the place of gender within diverse religious traditionalist, fundamentalist, or nationalist identity politics at the level of communities and movements within a global context - in other words, from the level of intra- to intercultural comparison. However problematic the application of often-used pejorative terms such as fundamentalism, it cannot be denied that a particular kind of patriarchal religious discourse is on the rise in culturally diverse forms, yet on a global scale. Typical of many of these movements appears to be the appropriation of certain aspects of 'modernity' and the rejection of others, most notably gender equality, which is perceived as a threat to the 'authentic' identity, religion or tradition. Whether 'tradition' is simply being continued – religious traditions such as Judaism being inherently and historically patriarchal from a feminist perspective – reproduced, adapted or reinvented, an increase in gender conservatism is no doubt taking place: 'Women, their roles, and above all their control, are at the heart of the fundamentalist agenda' (Sahgal and Yuval-Davis 1992a: 1), becoming both part and parcel of the community's identity.

In the shift from the first to the second main argument, and generally throughout the article, I have tried to give attention to nuances and have been wary of simple objectification and overgeneralisation, as in the 'false consciousness model' or 'women as victims' approach which characterised an earlier stage of feminist research on cross-cultural communities – and to some extent still does. Davidman's (1991) and Kaufman's (1993, 1994, 1995) studies of newly Orthodox women are precisely illustrative of a reactive trend in feminist research which moves beyond the victim approach in order to present more reflexive, fine-tuned, empathetic, and in general more feminist methodologically sound analyses of women's lives that are different to or probably almost the opposites of their interpreters. Feminist writers like Sahgal and Yuval-Davis (1992a), Sered (1992, 1999) and (Yuval-Davis 1992, 1999) are nonetheless critical of the apparent paradox that women who participate in fundamentalist movements – such as the Lubavitcher Hasidim – should actually 'gain a sense of empowerment within the spaces allocated to them by fundamentalist movements' (Sahgal and Yuval-Davis 1992a: 9).

Sered (1992), in a book review of Davidman (1991) and Kaufman (1993), for example, takes Kaufman to task for accepting her informants' point of view too easily and neglecting to compare their perceptions with actual practice, or including interviews with women who had more negative experiences under patriarchal law or left the Orthodox Jewish community. Yuval-Davis's (1992, 1999) own research on what she calls people who become *Khozrim Bitshuva* (returnees) among the Lubavitcher Hasidim is less extensive than that by Davidman and Kaufman, but nonetheless does portray the downside of the phenomenon, in line with her more general viewpoint on fundamentalism and its detrimental consequences for women's status. Despite all possible differences due to class position or other sociological determinants, the idea of empowerment for these women – e.g., emotional bonding between women in a separate women's community – remains problematic to the author. Besides the basic halakhic inequalities[18] that remain in place, some of the women and social workers Yuval-Davis interviewed reported cases of physical and mental exhaustion, postnatal depression among the poorer large families and other familial problems.

The more general paradox of empowerment and the necessity for a critical perspective revolves around the dilemma of identity politics of minorities or any kind of collectivities in general: 'Minority women often face the dilemma that the same particularistic collective identity that they seek to defend against racism and subordination, and from which they gain their empowerment to resist dominant oppressive systems and cultures, also oppresses them as women and can include many reactionary and exclusionary elements' (Yuval-

Davis 1999: 40). In my own interviews, even if the legitimising 'rhetoric of choice' was absent, the frum-born women I interviewed nevertheless perhaps did paint a rosy picture of their position as women within their traditionalist community. Although I did not make any enquiries about their financial status or 'class', the vast majority of the women living in Antwerp did appear to enjoy comfortable, some even affluent lifestyles, with domestic help for chores or help with the children when they were young. Speaking to me as an outsider, from their subject positions as 'spokespersons' for their relatively tiny minority community within a dominant secular and potentially racist modern society, I had not expected them to do any different than make this type of 'political' move. However, regardless of the political and theoretical shifts from both insensitivity to cultural and religious differences, and orientalist attitudes towards non-Western, secular, modern ways of life, towards a greater understanding of the reasons for and the diverse ways in which the construction of identities take place, feminists – among many others – are becoming increasingly critical of the essentialist consequences these relativist 'postmodern' (Moghissi 1999) or 'multicultural' (Cohen et al. 1999, Sahgal and Yuval-Davis 1992a) approaches in both theory and political practice seem to hold. Whilst in favour of (re)claiming 'gender' and 'identity' as nonessentialist and fruitful categories of analysis, by way of conclusion and political positioning I subscribe to this more critical note.

Notes

1. Sandra Harding (1986) proposes a similar multidimensional model of gender that must study the interaction between three levels of gender: gender symbolism, division of labour or gender structure and finally individual gender.
2. According to Heilman (1995: xxi) the haredim are today but a minority among a minority, some 25 percent of the 10 percent of Jews that self-identify as Orthodox. However, due to the growing assimilation and intermarriages among secular Jews, and their own high birth rate, both their absolute number and influence are growing. Novelist Robert Eisenbert (1996: 1) estimates that at an annual growth of 5 percent per year, hypothetically the 350,000 haredim of today will grow to a number between eight and ten million in 2075. Belcove-Shalin (1995a: 9) estimates the total number of Hasidim at 250,000 globally, of which 200,000 live in the U.S.
3. Exceptions are the pioneering ethnographic studies on Hasidim such as *Williamsburg: A Jewish Community in Transition* by George Kranzler (published in 1961) and *The Hasidic Community of Williamsburg: A Study in the Sociology of Religion* by Solomon Poll (published in 1962).
4. Harry Rabinowicz, *A World Apart: The Story of the Chasidim in Britain*, (1996). Laurence Podselver's (2000) contribution to a recent conference on Jewish women in the U.S. consists of a short account of her research among North African Lubavitch Hasidim in Paris. It is likely that similar studies, also on Sephardic Orthodox communities, have taken place, but here only the best known and widely distributed ethnographic monographs in the English language have been surveyed.
5. Written religious education for girls was first introduced in Eastern Europe during the second decade of the twentieth century (Morris 1998). In the Beit Ya'akov schools that were founded, girls followed a curriculum of subjects such as the Bible, Ethics, the code of Jewish Law, prayer, Commentaries and Hebrew grammar, all except for the study of the Talmud or the Oral Law, which remains the exclusive prerogative for boys and adult men. To this date, girls

in strictly Orthodox Jewish communities follow a similar, yet sophisticated curriculum, next to secular subjects, the latter often more extensive than the boys. Although there is historical and contemporary debate whether girls are halakhically exempt or even forbidden to study Talmud, for girls in traditionalist communities it is in any case deemed unnecessary for their proper role in life. This view was replicated by my own informants.

6. Tefillin are the two leather boxes containing scriptual passages that are bound to the left arm and on the head and worn during prayer. Tallit is the rectangular garment to which tzitzit, fringes, are attached, numbering 613, representing the mitzvot, the divine commandments.

7. The extent to which these laws of separation are put into practice depends on the community and its rabbinic authorities; the more traditionalist, the stricter the rules.

8. Details on the practical applications of the laws can be found in booklets and books written on the subject which are distributed or officially approved of by rabbinic authorities. As well as analyses of such manuals (e.g., Myers and Litman 1995, Steinberg 1997, Yanay and Rapoport 1997), I have also used publications distributed by the religious congregation Machsike Hadass in Antwerp, with which the strictly Orthodox Jewish women I interviewed are affiliated (Abramov 1988, Blasz 5752, Zahler 1980).

9. Bonnie Morris (1995, 1998) is another recent researcher on Lubavitcher women, using a more historical, textual approach rather than ethnography. Outside of the U.S., the only widely known and extensive ethnographic study that takes Hasidic women as the object of study can be attributed to the Israeli anthropologist Tamar El-Or (1994), whose monograph in Hebrew on women of the Gur Hasidim outside of Tel Aviv has been translated into English. Another smaller study of Hasidic women I have encountered has been conducted by Levine (1998) on Lubavitcher girls in Crown Heights. Yuval-Davis's (1992, 1999) research, which is partially based on research on Lubavitcher women, will be discussed in a later paragraph. Women researchers Belcove-Sahlin (1988) and Podselver (2000), who did not set out to focus only on women as ethnographic informants, nor take the issue of gender as the main focus in their research, have nevertheless both reflected on gender as a fundamental issue in the research process in terms of gaining entry to the lives of women and men as women researchers, although participant observation of ritual occasions such as study and prayer was more limited.

10. Davidman (1991) studies two distinct Orthodox communities who attract ba'alot teshuvah: a modern Orthodox synagogue and a Lubavitch Hasidic residential yeshiva. In the latter case Davidman herself stayed in the yeshiva in order to focus on the women in the process of conversion. Kaufman (1993) conducted in-depth interviews with 150 already converted and established ba'alot teshuvah in five major urban areas across the U.S. Twenty-five were modern Orthodox, eighty-five ultra-Orthodox (Hasidic) and forty strictly Orthodox women. The women mostly came from middle-class backgrounds, were well educated and had previously been assimilated into secular culture.

11. According to Abicht (1994: 70) some 42,000 Jews were officially registered in Belgium in 1942 and thousands of others were living there 'illegally'. Rabinowicz (1996: 39) claims some 100,000 Jews lived in Belgium, half of them living in the city of Antwerp, on the eve of the Second World War. As many as 24,811 Belgian Jewish children, women and men were deported to Auschwitz alone, of which 1,193 survived in 1945 (Abicht 1994: 70). The statistics of the Antwerp council do not register the religious or ethnic affiliation of the city's inhabitants, which means the only records available are the lists of members of religious congregations and other social and cultural services (Abicht 1988: 63, Abicht 1994: 134).

12. 'Gemeente van de Portugese Ritus', founded in 1910.

13. Personal communication from Julien Klener.

14. While most of the groups' rebbes live abroad, usually in Israel or the U.S., Antwerp has one court that has its own rebbe, the Przeworsker Hasidim. This dynasty was founded by Rebbe Isaac Gewirtsman from the Polish town of Prszeworsk, who came from Paris to Antwerp after the Second World War. In 1876 he was succeeded by his son Reb Jankel who, according to Rabinowicz (1996: 40), is currently 'the most charismatic rebbe in Europe'. Apparently, Reb Jankel was recently succeeded by his son Reb Leibisch (Rosenberg 1999).

15. The empirical data were supplemented by other material such as leaflets and literature on the role of women and Jewish family life and laws, which is distributed and sanctioned by the reli-

gious institutions of the community itself, and manuals on the laws of family purity. In addition, secondary literature such as novels, which are widely read by women within the community, were analysed.

16. Coincidence or not, although I did not intentionally set out not to interview any Lubavitcher women (a community which is also represented in Antwerp), I did not succeed in contacting any, nor was I referred to any Lubavitcher women by other Hasidic women. Another factor which may be relevant is that the greater part of the research on traditional Jewish communities, known to me, has been carried out by – mostly secular – Jewish researchers. This may account for a possible advantage in approaching the Lubavitcher, as the researchers may be perceived as potential 'returnees'.

17. A monographic type of study by political correspondent David Landau (1993) of the Haredim in New York, London and Jerusalem, by contrast, does explicitly feature the term fundamentalism.

18. Besides the already noted exclusion of religious public service, study and positions of authority, the most notable include not being allowed to serve as a witness in religious courts, and the impossibility of obtaining a religious divorce (the problem of the *get*) against the will of the husband.

Bibliography

Abicht, Ludo. 1988. *De Joden van Antwerpen*. Brussel: Grammens.

————— 1994. *De joden van België*. Amsterdam and Antwerpen: Uitgeverij Atlas.

Abramov, Tehilla. 1988. *The Secret of Jewish Femininity: Insights into the Practice of Taharat HaMischpachah*. Southfield, Mich.: Targum Press.

Alcoff, Linda and Potter, Elizabeth. 1993. 'Introduction: When Feminisms Intersect Epistemology'. In *Feminist Epistemologies*, eds. Linda Alcoff and Elizabeth Potter, 1–14. New York and London: Routledge.

Armstrong, Karen. 2000. *De strijd om God. Een geschiedenis van het fundamentalisme* (transl. of *The Battle for God*). Amsterdam: De Bezige Bij.

Belcove-Shalin, Janet S. 1988. 'Becoming More of an Eskimo. Fieldwork among the Hasidim of Boro Park'. In *Between Two Worlds. Ethnographic Essays on American Jewry*, ed. Jack Kugelmass, 77–102. Ithaca and London: Cornell University Press.

————— 1995a. 'Introduction. New World Hasidim'. In *New World Hasidim: Ethnographic Studies of Hasidic Jews in America*, ed. Janet S. Belcove-Shalin, 1–30. Albany: State University of New York Press.

————— (ed.) 1995b. *New World Hasidim: Ethnographic Studies of Hasidic Jews in America*. Albany: State University of New York Press.

Blasz, Rabbin Elyohu 5752. 'Code de la Pureté Familiale Juive'. *Un condensé des lois de Nidda sous forme abrégée*, 5th edn. Monsey, N.Y.: Comité de la Pureté Familiale Juive.

Bok, Willy. 1986. 'Verstrengeling van het godsdienstige en het wereldlijke in de Belgische joodse milieus', *Tijdschrift voor Sociologie*, No. 7: 365–79.

Bourdieu, Pierre. 2001. *Masculine Domination*. Cambridge: Polity Press.

Brah, Avtar. 1996. *Cartographies of Diaspora: Contesting Identities*. London and New York: Routledge.

Braidotti, Rosi. 1994. *Nomadic Subjects: Embodiment and Sexual Difference in Contemporary Feminist Theory*. New York: Columbia University Press.

Brouns, Margo. 1995. 'Feminisme en wetenschap'. In *Vrouwenstudies in de jaren negentig. Een kennismaking vanuit verschillende disciplines*, eds. Margo Brouns, Mieke Verloo and Marianne Grünell, 11–27. Bussum: Dick Coutinho.

Butler, Judith. 1990a. *Gender Trouble. Feminism and the Subversion of Identity*. New York
    and London: Routledge.
———— 1990b. 'Gender Trouble, Feminist Theory, and Psychoanalytic Discourse'. In
    Feminism/Postmodernism, ed. Linda J. Nicholson, 324–40. New York and London:
    Routledge.
———— 1992. 'Contingent Foundations: Feminism and the Question of
    "Postmodernism"'. In *Feminists Theorize the Political*, eds. Judith Butler and Joan
    W. Scott, 3–21. New York and London: Routledge.
———— and Scott, Joan W. (eds.) 1992. *Feminists Theorize the Political*. New York and
    London: Routledge.
Bynum, Caroline Walker. 1986. 'Introduction: The Complexity of Symbols'. In *Gender
    and Religion: On the Complexity of Symbols*, eds. Caroline W. Bynum, Stevan Harrell
    and Paula Richman, 1–20. Boston, Mass.: Beacon Press.
Charles, Nickie and Hintjens Helen (eds.) 1998. *Gender, Ethnicity and Political Ideologies*.
    London and New York: Routledge.
Chodorow, Nancy. 1978. *The Reproduction of Mothering*. Berkeley: University of Califor-
    nia Press.
Cohen, Joshua, Howard, Matthew and Nussbaum, Martha C. (eds.) 1999. Is *Multicul-
    turalism Bad for Women? Susan Moller Okin with Respondents*. Princeton, N.J.: Prince-
    ton University Press.
Cromer, Gerald. 1993. 'Withdrawal and Conquest: Two Aspects of the Haredi Reponse
    to Modernity'. In *Jewish Fundamentalism in Comparative Perspective. Religion, Ideol-
    ogy, and the Crisis of Modernity*, ed. Laurence J. Silberstein, 164–80. New York and
    London: New York University Press.
Davidman, Lynn. 1991. *Tradition in a Rootless World: Women Turn to Orthodox Judaism*.
    Berkeley, Los Angeles and Oxford: University of California Press.
Eisenberg, Robert. 1996. *Boychicks in the Hood: Travels in the Hasidic Underground*. Lon-
    don: Quartet Books.
El-Or, Tamar. 1994. *Educated and Ignorant: Ultraorthodox Jewish Women and Their World*.
    Boulder and London: Lynne Rienner Publications.
Ferree, Myra Marx, Lorber, Judith and Hess, Beth B. 1999. 'Introduction'. In *Revisioning
    Gender*, eds. Myra Marx Ferree, Judith Lorber and Beth B. Hess, xv–xxxvi. Thousand
    Oaks, London and New Delhi: Sage Publications.
Frankiel, Tamar. 1990. *The Voice of Sarah: Feminine Spirituality and Traditional Judaism*.
    New York: Biblio Press.
Fraser, Nancy and Nicholson, Linda J. 1990. 'Social Criticism without Philosophy. An
    Encounter between Feminism and Postmodernism'. In *Feminism/Postmodernism*, ed.
    Linda J. Nicholson, 19–38. New York and London: Routledge.
Friedman, Menachem. 1993. 'Jewish Zealots. Conservative versus Innovative'. In *Jewish
    Fundamentalism in Comparative Perspective: Religion, Ideology and the Crisis of Moder-
    nity*, ed. Laurence J. Silberstein, 148–63. New York and London: New York Univer-
    sity Press.
Greenberg, Blu. 1998. *On Women and Judaism: A View from Tradition*. Philadelphia and
    Jerusalem: The Jewish Publication Society of America (orig. 1981).
Gilligan, Carol. 1982. *In a Different Voice*. Cambridge and London: Harvard University
    Press.
———— 1997. 'In a Different Voice: Women's Conceptions of Self and Morality'. In
    Feminist Social Thought. A Reader, ed. Diana Tietjens Meyers, 549–82. New York
    and London: Routledge (orig. in *Harvard Educational Review*, 47:4, 1977, 481–517).

Gross, Rita M. 1977. 'Androcentrism and Androgyny in the Methodology of History of Religions'. In *Beyond Androcentrism: New Essays on Women and Religion*, ed. Rita M. Gross, 7–19. Missoula, Montana: Scholars Press.

Gutwirth, Jacques. 1968. 'Antwerp Jewry Today', *The Jewish Journal of Sociology*, Vol. 10, No. 1: 121–37 (revised version of 'Le Judaïsme anversoise aujourd'hui', *Revue des Etudes Juives,* Vol. 125, No. 4, 1966).

————— 1970. *Vie Juive Traditionelle. Ethnologie d'une communauté Hassidique*. Paris: Les Editions de Minuit.

————— 1999. 'Een halve eeuw herleving van het chassidisme', *Streven*, July–August, 603–14.

Haraway, Donna. 1988. 'Situated Knowledges. The Science Question in Feminism and the Privilege of Partial Perspective', *Feminist Studies*, Vol. 14, No. 3: 575–99.

Harding, Sandra. 1986. *The Science Question in Feminism*. Ithaca, New York: Cornell University Press.

————— 1991. *Whose Science? Whose Knowledge? Thinking from Women's Lives*. Ithaca, New York: Cornell University Press.

Harris, Lis. 1995. *Holy Days: The World of a Hasidic Family.* New York, London, Toronto, Sydney, Tokyo and Singapore: Simon and Schuster (orig. 1985).

Heilman, Samuel C. 1992. *Defenders of the Faith: Inside Ultra-Orthodox Jewry*. New York: Schocken Books.

————— 1995. 'Foreword'. In *New World Hasidim. Ethnographic Studies of Hasidic Jews in America*, ed. Janet S. Belcove-Shalin, xi–xv. Albany: State University of New York Press.

————— and Friedman, Menachem. 1991. 'Religious Fundamentalism and Religious Jews. The Case of the Haredim'. In *Fundamentalisms Observed*, eds. Martin E. Marty and Scott R. Appleby, 197–264. Chicago, IU.: University of Chicago Press.

Howland, Courtney W. (ed.) 1999. *Religious Fundamentalisms and the Human Rights of Women*. Basingstoke: Macmillan Press.

Hyman, Paula E. 1999. 'A Feminist Perspective on Jewish Fundamentalism'. In *Religious Fundamentalisms and the Human Rights of Women*, ed. Courtney W. Howland, 271–80. Basingstoke: Macmillan Press.

Katchadourian, Herant A. 1979. 'The Terminology of Sex and Gender'. In *Human Sexuality. A Comparative and Developmental Perspective,* ed., Herant A. Katchadourian, 8–34. Berkeley, Los Angeles and London: University of California Press.

Kaufman, Debra Renee. 1993. *Rachel's Daughters: Newly Orthodox Jewish Women*. New Brunswick, N.J.: Rutgers University Press.

————— 1994. 'Paradoxical Politics. Gender Politics Among Newly Orthodox Jewish Women in the United States'. In *Identity Politics and Women: Cultural Reassertions and Feminisms in International Perspective*, ed. Valentine M. Moghadam, 349–66. Boulder, San Francisco and Oxford: Westview Press.

————— 1995. 'Engendering Orthodoxy: Newly Orthodox Women and Hasidim'. In New World Hasidim. Ethnographic Studies of Hasidic Jews in America, ed. Janet S. Belcove-Shalin, 135–60. Albany: State University of New York Press.

Kaufman, Michael. 1995. *The Woman in Jewish Law and Tradition*. Northvale, New Jersey and London: Jason Aronson Inc.

King, Ursula. 1995. 'Introduction. Gender and the Study of Religion'. In *Religion and Gender*, ed. Ursula King, 1–38. Oxford: Blackwell.

Kranzler, George. 1961. Williamsburg, A Jewish Community in Transition. New York: Philipp Feldheim.

————— 1995. *Hasidic Williamsburg: A Contemporary American Hasidic Community.* Northvale, New Jersey and London: Jason Aronson Inc.

Landau, David. 1993. *Piety and Power: The World of Jewish Fundamentalism*. London: Secker and Warburg.

Levine, Stephanie. 1998. 'Hasidic Girls. Daily Lives and Inner Worlds'. In *Millennium Girls: Today's Girls around the World*, ed. Sherrie A. Inness, 61–86. Lanham, Boulder, New York and Oxford: Rowman and Littlefield Publishers.

Lustick, Ian S. 1993. 'Jewish Fundamentalism and the Israeli–Palestinian Impasse'. In *Jewish Fundamentalism in Comparative Perspective: Religion, Ideology, and the Crisis of Modernity*, ed. Laurence J. Silberstein, 104–16. New York and London: New York University Press.

Manning, Christel. 1999. *God Gave Us the Right: Conservative Catholic, Evangelical Protestant, and Orthodox Jewish Women Grapple with Feminism*. Brunswick, New Jersey and London: Rutgers University Press.

Martin, M. Kay and Voorhies, Barbara 1975. *Female of the Species*. New York: Columbia University Press.

Mead, Margaret. 1963. *Sex and Temperament in Three Primitive Societies*. New York: William Morrow (orig. 1935).

Meijers, Daniel. 1992. *Ascetic Hasidism in Jerusalem: The Guardian-Of-The-Faithful Community of Mea Shearim*. Leiden, New York, Kobenhavn and Köln: E.J. Brill.

Mintz, Jerome R. 1994. *Hasidic People: A Place in the New World*. Cambridge, Mass. and London, England: Harvard University Press.

Moghadam, Valentine M. (ed.) 1994a. *Identity Politics and Women. Cultural Reassertions and Feminisms in International Perspective*. Boulder, San Francisco and Oxford: Westview Press.

—— 1994b. 'Women and Identity Politics in Theoretical and Comparative Perspective'. In *Identity Politics and Women: Cultural Reassertions and Feminisms in International Perspective*, ed. Valentine M. Moghadam, 3–26. Boulder, San Francisco and Oxford: Westview Press.

Moghissi, Haideh. 1999. *Feminism and Islamic Fundamentalism: The Limits of Postmodern Analysis*. London and New York: Zed Books.

Moore, Henrietta L. 1993. 'The Differences Within and the Differences Between'. In *Gendered Anthropology*, ed. Teresa del Valle, 193–204. London and New York: Routledge.

—— 1994a. '"Divided We Stand". Sex, Gender and Sexual Difference', *Feminist Review*, No. 47: 78–95.

—— 1994b. *A Passion for Difference: Essays in Anthropology and Gender*. Cambridge: Polity Press.

—— 1999. 'Whatever Happened to Women and Men? Gender and other Crises in Anthropology'. In *Anthropological Theory Today,* ed. Henrietta L. Moore, 151–71. Cambridge: Polity Press.

Morris, Bonnie J. 1995. 'Agents or Victims of Religious Ideology? Approaches to Locating Hasidic Women in Feminist Studies'. In *New World Hasidim. Ethnographic Studies of Hasidic Jews in America*, ed. Janet S. Belcove-Sahlin, 161–80. Albany: State University of New York Press.

—— 1998. *Lubavitcher Women in America. Identity and Activism in the Postwar Era*. Albany: State University of New York Press.

Morris, Rosalind C. 1995. 'All Made Up. Performance Theory and the New Anthropology of Sex and Gender', *Annual Review of Anthropology*, Vol. 24: 567–92.

Myers, Jody and Litman, Jane Rachel 1995. 'The Secret of Jewish Femininity. Hiddenness, Power, and Physicality in the Theology of Orthodox Women in the Contemporary World'. In *Gender and Judaism: The Transformation of Tradition*, ed. T.M. Rudavsky, 51–77. New York and London: New York University Press.

Oakley, Ann. 1996. *Sex, Gender and Society*. 2nd edition. Aldershot: Arena.

Ortner, Sherry B. and Whitehead, Harriet (eds.) 1981. *Sexual Meanings: The Cultural Construction of Gender and Sexuality*. Cambridge, London, New York, New Rochelle, Melbourne and Sydney: Cambridge University Press.

Podselver, Laurence. 2000. 'Teshuvah Among French Jewish Women'. In *Jewish Women 2000: Conference Papers from the HRIJW International Scholarly Exchanges 1997–1998*, ed. Helena Epstein, 161–67. *The Hadassah Research Institute on Jewish Women*.

Poll, Solomon. 1962. *The Hasidic Community of Williamsburg: A Study in the Sociology of Religion*. New York: Schocken Books.

Rabonowicz, Harry. 1996. *A World Apart: The Story of Chassidim in England*. London: Vallentine Mitchell.

Rabinowicz, Tzvi M. 1996. *The Encyclopedia of Hasidism*. Northvale, New Jersey and London: Jason Aronson Inc.

Riley, Denise. 1988. *'Am I That Name?' Feminism and the Category of 'Women' in History*. London: Macmillan.

———— 'A Short History of Some Preoccupations'. In *Feminists Theorize the Political*, eds. Judith Butler and Joan W. Scott, 121–29. New York and London: Routledge.

Rosenberg, Henri. 1999. 'Jewish Organizations of Antwerp', http://www.jewishantwerp.com/ JewOrgan.htm

———— 2000. 'Machsike Hadass versus Shomrei Hadass', http://www.lawyer-a1.com/Articles.htm

Saerens, Lieven. 2000. *Vreemdelingen in een wereldstad. Een geschiedenis van Antwerpen en zijn joodse bevolking (1880–1944)*. Tielt: Lannoo.

Sahgal, Gita and Nira Yuval-Davis. 1992a. 'Introduction. Fundamentalism, Multiculturalism and Women in Britain'. In *Refusing Holy Orders. Women and Fundamentalism in Britain*, eds. Gita Sahgal and Nira Yuval-Davis, 1–25. London: Virago Press.

———— (eds.) 1992b. *Refusing Holy Orders: Women and Fundamentalism in Britain*. London: Virago Press.

Sanday, Peggy Reeves and Goodenough, Ruth Gallagher, (eds.) 1990. *Beyond the Second Sex: New Directions in the Anthropology of Gender*. Philadelphia: University of Pennsylvania Press.

Scott, Joan W. 1996. 'Gender: A Useful Category of Historical Analysis'. In *Feminism and History*, ed. Joan W. Scott, 152–80. Oxford and New York: Oxford University Press.

Sered, Susan Starr. 1992. 'Book Reviews. Rachel's Daughters; Tradition in a Rootless World', *Journal for the Scientific Study of Religion*, Vol. 31, No. 3: 385–87.

———— 1998. 'De-Gendering Religious Leadership. Sociological Discourse in an Okinawan Village', *Journal of the American Academy of Religion*, Vol. 66, No. 3: 589–611.

———— 1999. '"Woman" as Symbol and Women as Agents. Gendered Religious Discourses and Practices'. In *Revisioning Gender*, eds. Myra Marx Ferree, Judith Lorber and Beth B. Hess, 193–221. Thousand Oaks, London and New Delhi: Sage Publications.

Silberstein, Laurence J. (1993). 'Religion, Ideology, Modernity. Theoretical Issues in the Study of Jewish Fundamentalism'. In *Jewish Fundamentalism in Comparative Perspective: Religion, Ideology, and the Crisis of Modernity*, ed. Laurence J. Silberstein, 3–26. New York and London: New York University Press.

Stacey, Judith and Barrie Thorne. 1998. 'The Missing Feminist Revolution in Sociology'. In *Feminist Foundations. Toward Transforming Sociology*, eds. Kristen A. Myers, Cynthia D. Anderson and Barbara J. Risman, 219–39. Thousand Oaks, London and New Delhi: Sage Publications.

Stanley, Liz and Wise, Sue. 1990. 'Method, Methodology and Epistemology in Feminist Research'. In *Feminist Praxis: Research, Theory and Epistemology in Feminist Sociology*, ed. Liz Stanley, 20–59. London and New York: Routledge.

Steinberg, Jonah. 1997. 'From a "Pot of Filth" to a "Hedge of Roses" (and Back). Changing Theorizations of Menstruation in Judaism', *Journal of Feminist Studies in Religion*, Vol. 13, No. 2: 5–26.

Stump, Roger W. 2000. *Boundaries of Faith: Geographical Perspectives on Religious Fundamentalism*. Lanham, Boulder, New York and Oxford: Rowman and Littlefield Publishers.

Webber, Jonathan. 1987. 'Rethinking Fundamentalism. The Readjustment of Jewish Society in the Modern World'. In *Studies in Religious Fundamentalism*, ed. Lionel Caplan, 95–121. Hampshire and London: Macmillan Press.

────── 1994. 'Introduction'. In *Jewish Identities in the New Europe*, ed. Jonathan Webber, 1–32. London and Washington: Littman Library of Jewish Civilization.

────── 1997. 'Jews and Judaism in Contemporary Europe? Religion or Ethnic Group?', *Ethnic and Racial Studies*, Vol. 20, No. 2: 257–79.

Weir, Alison. 1996. *Sacrificial Logics: Feminist Theory and the Critique of Identity*. New York and London: Routledge.

West, Candace and Zimmerman, Don H. 1987. 'Doing Gender', *Gender and Society*, Vol.1: 125–51.

Yanagisako, Sylvia and Collier, Jane F. 1987. 'Toward a Unified Analysis of Gender and Kinship'. In *Gender and Kinship: Essays Toward a Unified Analysis*, eds. Jane F. Collier and Sylvia Yanagisako, 14–50. Stanford, Cal.: Stanford University Press.

────── 1990. 'The Mode of Reproduction'. In *Theoretical Perspectives on Sexual Difference*, ed. Deborah L. Rhode, 131–41. Binghamton, N.Y.: Vail-Ballou Press.

Yanay, Niza and Rapoport, Tamar. 1997. 'Ritual Impurity and Religious Discourse on Women and Nationality', *Women's Studies International Forum*, Vol. 20, No. 5/6: 651–63.

Yuval-Davis, Nira. 1992. 'Jewish Fundamentalism and Women's Empowerment'. In *Refusing Holy Orders: Women and Fundamentalism in Britain*, eds. Gita Sahgal and Nira Yuval-Davis, 198–226. London: Virago Press

────── 1997. *Gender and Nation*. London, Thousand Oaks and New Delhi: Sage Publications.

────── 1999. 'The Personal is Political. Jewish Fundamentalism and Women's Empowerment'. In *Religious Fundamentalisms and the Human Rights of Women*, ed. Courtney W. Howland, 33–42. Basingstoke: Macmillan Press.

Zahler, Rabbijn Zwi. 1980. *De reinheid van het joodse huwelijk. Taharat Hammisjpacha*. Antwerpen: Tseïreï Agudas Chabad.

3

FIVE CENTURIES OF COMPELLING INTERCULTURALITY: THE INDIAN IN LATIN-AMERICAN CONSCIOUSNESS

Koen De Munter

> *Arauco feels a sorrow I cannot keep silent about. It is about*
> *centuries-old injustices, that all can see applied,*
> *yet no one did repair it, even when being*
> *able to do so. So rise, Huenchullán…*
> Violeta Parra[1]

A Contemporary Aymara in Urban El Alto (Bolivia)

Don Casto Choque, nowadays a senior Aymara *residente* in El Alto, located on the barren Altiplano just above the capital La Paz, came for the first time to the city on a day in 1960. Then a young boy living in a small indigenous community near the shores of the lake Titicaca, he was accompanying some older relatives who were carrying Peruvian 'contraband' to sell in La Paz ('in the darkness of the night all of a sudden we collided with the air of the city…'). El Alto in those days was still a small, poorly articulated conglomerate of a handful of former *comunidades originarias* that were doomed 'to become a city',[2] as had sounded the official verdict a decade before. Forty years later, and due to massive migration from the countryside, El Alto – *Altupata* as they call it in Aymara – has become a big, indigenous city with almost three-quarters of a million inhabitants (in a country of eight million people). For a long time it was considered as a kind of Cinderella-appendix to La Paz, but since the 1990s it has slowly gained its own autonomy. Culturally, the people living in El Alto have given birth to an intriguing interaction of urban 'homes abroad' *within* the traditional habitat of the Altiplano.

Don Casto settled in El Alto with his family around 1980, after several years of tough experiences in downtown La Paz while working in family-run, informal textile manufacturing. In El Alto he managed to earn a living with relatives in a similar informal way, manufacturing clothes with fabric woven on fifty-year-old mechanical looms, imported and recycled from 'China'. Repeating the label Aymara – Indian – people have pinned on them by the hegemonic *criollos*, he often called himself a *sonso* or stupid (...Indian) during our conversations on his life story. He would say this because now he knows that in the course of his life he has been seriously deceived or misunderstood, for instance by the (foreign) evangelical missionaries under whose spell he fell as a youngster in the countryside or by the false – and possibly fake – city lawyer who swindled his family when they wanted to provide for their lands in the *comunidad*. He feels deceived by the hospital doctor with whom communication is almost non-existent and who never listens or does not even respect don Casto's own paratactic ways of 'explaining' the 'illnesses'. He also feels betrayed by the current rulers who, in spite of certain nice promises, keep on ignoring their *cultura originaria* and who, as always, have their eyes on anything that comes from abroad, from *gringolandia*. Via a trade union broadsheet he got to know that these *gringos* come to the country to squeeze everything to their own benefit.

Fifty-year-old don Casto considers himself 'stupid', but next to his bed lies an anatomy atlas and at the same time he is studying the use of medicinal herbs.In addition, he likes to inform himself by comparing the different radio stations on the content of their broadcasts. During one of the last elections he refused to vote because 'there are no more real communists anymore', and because 'politicians treat people as dogs which they keep quiet for a while by giving them a bone'. At the same time, though, he passionately kept on following election results. In addition to this, in his rural home community he is assuming one of the traditional authority roles, namely *alcalde escolar*, in being responsible for the small local school.

The Indian in Latin-American Conscience

Some five hundred years ago (for the Andean cultures actually since 1532) the Spanish *Conquista*, that impressively obtrusive invasion of Christian Western European culture into the 'empty' continent, was about to provoke a massive encounter between two Others, two different cultural spheres which had never met before, not even indirectly. We know how it all started with Christopher Columbus's orientation mistake(s) and divine conceit. Sadly enough, misunderstanding and destructive arrogance would keep on determining the rhythm of further interactions between the hegemonic colonisers and colonised indigenous peoples in the Americas.

Undoubtedly, Columbus, driven by what Tzvetan Todorov once called 'medieval-Christian dreams', unleashed an irreversible process of intense – though brutally unequal –contacts between Western cultures and a range of indigenous cultural groups (that were never or rarely going to be recognised in their amazing heterogeneity). The history of Latin America presents us with a splendid – but stark – exercise in the interaction of antagonistic cultures. That is precisely why Todorov (1982), as he explains in the introduction to his sharp *La conquête de l'Amérique. La question de l'autre*, chose the history of sixteenth-century 'America' as an *histoire exemplaire* for his general reflections on (Western?) relationships with the Other.[3] Todorov might be criticised in terms of an intellectually unfortunate ethnocentrism, when he asserts that the Spaniards could conquer quite easily because they actually *understood* the indigenous Other *better* than vice versa (Subirats 1994). Nonetheless, it is to Todorov's merit to have shown how the 'marvellous encounter' basically meant 'the biggest genocide in human history'. This multiple genocide of cultures, this destruction of historical forms by the 'logic of colonisation' was fortunately not complete. But the colonial relationships, globally and locally entwined, remain violent up until this day.[4]

As anthropologists we may then ask ourselves what those five centuries of conflicting cohabitation have brought about on the level of cultural dynamics and identities. We will first address this general question by tackling the central issue of the *mestizaje cultural*, appearing throughout Latin America as a metaphor and as an ideology. Different kinds of narratives about the so-called uniquely mixed culture (and nature) have contributed to political and intellectual power in Latin America, marginalising the ongoing, significant presence of indigenous groups. Secondly, this question will be approached by way of a brief evaluation and critique of the work of two important contemporary Latin-American thinkers on the relationship between identities and modernity in their continent, Jorge Larraín Ibáñez and Néstor García Canclini. Thirdly, we shall relate these approaches to our own anthropological fieldwork among the urban Aymara in Bolivia, bringing the question back to concrete indigenous pro-gression.

Given the fact that, in spite of the destructive 'logic of colonisation', indigenous people have been an important motor of the cultural mestizaje-process ever since the Invasion, a second, more concrete question arises, namely up to what point, and in which sense, this indigenous, 'Indian part' is at present really being allowed to become part of 'Latin-American' consciousness, practices, curricula, and so on. 'Latin America' is, of course, an extremely heterogeneous and, in a certain way, imaginary whole, with different cultural constellations between and within the respective national settings. For instance, the southernmost countries – Argentina, Chile and Uruguay, the so-called *Cono Sur* – are mainly determined by European immigration, and only recently has attention been given to the native cultures. In Chile, for example, where some important indigenous cultural groups have managed to survive, these groups were for a long time totally ignored in educational curricula (the contrary happened with the Western 'mother cultures'(!); they are still studied and revered as the superior cultural matrices, while there is not a single word about the 'own' cultural horizon, Tiwanaku). In those countries which still have large groups of indigenous people (Bolivia, Ecuador, Guatemala, Mexico[5] and Perú), the dominant white castes usually, and almost as a matter of course, consider these groups as an obstacle to progress and modernity. At best, these same ruling groups manipulate them in opportunistic ways in the margins of the general discourse on mestizo-normativity. Because it has become internationally fashionable – superficially correct – a certain indigenous-minded wind seems to blow now and then in public discourses. In such cases, it almost always concerns the rather small, innocent groups, not the potentially dangerous masses that migrated – and still migrate – to the big cities, or the protesting, organising and marching *campesinos*.[6] The sinuous ways in which the Mexican government has been treating the Zapatista-EZLN demands points in the same direction.

The indigenous cultural groups that survived have been subjected to different dynamics. The beddings of these cultural processes have become broader, more crossing and less clear. They show a complexity that is increasingly interwoven with a certain 'Western' way of life, but that, at the same time, seems to remain stubbornly creative and inventive.

Despite all the differences within the imagined Latin America – neither the intriguing Caribbean region, nor complex cases such as Colombia and Venezuela have been considered – it makes sense to consider indigenous progression within a 'Latin-American' scope, precisely because reference to a Latin-American identity (founded, basically, on shared hegemonic religion and language through the historical Conquista, and with a growing focus on the central theme of mestizaje) in intellectually and politically dominant circles has grown continuously in the twentieth century (nevertheless, the issue of indigenous participation has remained unaddressed). Drawing on our anthropological experience, we shall focus here on the evolution in the Spanish-speaking Latin-American region, more exactly the Andean region. Nevertheless, the Brazilian situation (with the Portuguese colonisation) could also, in a universalising approach, be taken into consideration.

Mestizaje Cultural, Mestizaje Económico

Since the beginning of the 1990s, and especially since the emblematic year 1992, there has been a great deal of discussion in Spain and Latin America about the specific character of cultural mestizaje. Some refer to a great process of cultural synthesis as a result of Spanish interference. The shamelessly aestheticising rhetoric of the Venezuelan writer Arturo Uslar Prieti is but one sad example of this approach (see his recent collection of essays under the fallacious title *La invención de América Mestiza,* 1997). Simultaneously, an (un)official think tank in Spain continues to emphasise the region's 'European identity' – flying in the face of its obvious but unwelcome North-African heritage – referring proudly and even haughty to Spain's civilising achievements in Latin America. No less striking, in this respect, was the optimistic and conceited discourse on mestizaje that characterised many Latin-American and particularly Mexican intellectuals at the beginning of the 1990s. Mexico, in particular, has always used mestizaje as the central metaphor for a national project. One of the leading voices in the revival of mestizaje discourse was the Mexican writer, Carlos Fuentes. In the run-up to the 1992 celebrations, he highlighted the importance of mestizaje for Europe in the twenty-first century, asserting that the experience of dealing with the Other would be of capital importance in a world that is increasingly multicultural. According to Fuentes: 'Fortunately it was not the English but the Spanish which came here (we [!, sic] did not put the Indians in reservations, slavery was abolished a lot earlier, etc.), because in that case we would not have had what we will need for the XXIst century: the experience of *mestizaje*.'[8]

Elsewhere I have interpreted similar demagogic, hispanophile and almost arrogant visions as part of an 'ideology of mestizaje', by means of which the indecent conditions of cultural interaction in Latin America were glossed over in an unacceptable way. The neo-Zapatista revolution in Chiapas would later lead persons such as Fuentes to somehow dissociate themselves from this mystifying belief in the mestizaje enterprise. In general, however, mestizaje (cultural) has remained the happy-ending success story, obstructing a closer look at what really has been at stake from the vantage point of indigenous progression during those centuries of intriguing and compelling cultural interaction, beneath *la historia oficial*.

Fortunately, there are also works that discuss this clash of cultures quite differently, even though they have not received the same attention. A beautiful example is *El universo mental de la conquista de América*, by the Peruvian Nelson Manrique (1993). Writing from the other continent, Manrique analyses the Spanish Conquista mentality, with its suppressed Jewish-Moorish component, and lays bare the colonial matrix of racism in general. Another commendable publication was *Esas Yndias equivocadas y malditas*, by the Spanish writer Rafael Sánchez Ferlosio (1994). His book is one massive, cutting attack on the Spanish conquering enterprise. Sánchez Ferlioso argues that historically, rather than mestizaje, one ought to speak about a multiple violation. This book was written to be published in 1992, as a counterweight to the victorious anniversary tone, but was not accepted at the time by the mainstream editorial houses. It was only published in 1994, also the year of publication of that brilliant masterpiece of Spanish historical self-critique, *El continente vacío* (The empty continent), by the polemical Spanish philosopher, Eduardo Subirats. Subirats's (1994) interests go beyond an attack on the Conquista itself. His book develops an interesting perspective on the *lógica de la colonización* that went hand in hand with the destruction of the historical forms of indigenous groups. This allows him to fiercely criticise every 'indigenista' perspective inclined towards reconciliation (he mentions, amongst others, the sacred León Portilla), if it does not constantly recognise and remind us of that terrible process of historical and cultural emptying (followed by a 'filling up' with values deemed to be universal). Although I am sympathetic to Subirats's lucid reading of colonial and postcolonial history in the Americas, his vision must be complemented by an anthropological perspective that focuses on the complex dynamics of survival and resistance taking place *within* indigenous pro-gression. For the destruction of historical forms, however terrible it may have been, did not manage to wipe out indigenous memory and practices.

My own approach to mestizaje drew on the work of the Peruvian writer and anthropologist, José María Arguedas (1911–69). More than developing a general philosophical or ethno-historical approach to that harsh encounter, Arguedas attempted, through novels and anthropological studies, to follow as closely as possible the great societal changes taking place during the twentieth century in Perú and in all of Latin America.

Arguedas himself poignantly embodies the conflict between the two antagonistic cultural identities, the Western and the indigenous (in his case the Quechua) ways-of-dealing-with-the-world. Although born in a white-class setting at the beginning of the twentieth century, Arguedas was raised by Quechua Indians because of dramatic family circumstances. Thus, he learnt the Quechua language and life poetics at a very early age. Later on, his father put him back on the Western path by sending him to a Jesuit school. Afterwards, Arguedas studied literature and anthropology at the San Marcos University in Lima (where he would later lecture in anthropology). He used both disciplines to get a better understanding of what was happening to his beloved indigenous cultures. Following both paths, Arguedas committed himself passionately to these cultural groups, which were increasingly threatened by modernity.

The impact of modernity (new roads, explosion of the urban centres, burgeoning industry in the coastal region) in Perú had increased remarkably since the 1940s and was about to have a definitive, disturbing effect on the cultural organisation of the traditional communities in the rural Andes region. Arguedas's vision on indigenous history can be summarised by saying that, until the beginning of the twentieth century, the Andean and Spanish cultures had interacted in important ways, albeit that this interplay had been constantly limited by the extremely unjust balance of power of the colony. It is to Arguedas's credit that from the very beginning he defended and admired (in the 1930s with the rather superficially 'indígena-minded' *indigenismo*-movement) the 'mixed artefacts' produced through centuries of mutual influence in agriculture, music and religion. Anthropologically, this position was later connected with his interest in the 'new *mestizos*', young indigenous people who looked both critically and respectfully at their own tradition and communities. They evolved through acts and strategies, combining these more swiftly than anyone – themselves included – could realise or understand, thereby moving away from a suffocating authenticity discourse and from assimilation-acculturation discourse. He regarded their 'intercultural capacities' as a possible key to the enduring feasibility of indigenous cultural tradition (or identity, understanding both as processes), while remaining well aware of the constant danger of uprootedness.

Things were not so simple, after all. Arguedas argued that, in spite of that century-long interaction, both cultural spheres had evolved following mainly separate ways, divided by what he called 'an irreconcilable difference between the economical concepts of both cultures'. The Western concepts of labour and property were – and still are – mercantile and individualistic; the Quechua counterparts had remained collectivist and religious.[9] Thanks to modernity, Western economy advanced brutally and definitively affected the sheltering divide. In the course of fieldwork in the 1940s, carried out in a rural Peruvian region with a specific historical evolution, Arguedas discovered that native communities were able to keep their cultural tradition flourishing thanks to an economically flexible attitude that took account of the burgeoning market economy. He also took a gloomy view of the situation of the very traditional, closed communities, determined by rigid social frameworks. This enabled him to formulate his economical and emancipatory definition of the mestizo:[10] 'As soon as the Indian, because of special circumstances, comes to understand this aspect of Western culture, as soon as he weapons himself with it and deals with it, he becomes a mestizo and a factor of positive [culturally spoken] economic production' (Arguedas 1976: 25). The *indios* would manage to adapt themselves and maintain their cultural progression by this insight, not by other, more superficial cultural elements.

Arguedas understood that changes were taking place very swiftly, and he advocated registering as quickly as possible all traditional forms of wisdom and society-building (*antropología de la urgencia*), before they were destroyed. His conception of an urgent anthropology was not fatalist, however. By registering these traditional forms of wisdom and society-building, the indigenous people would be able to support and inspire their own process of adaptation. Culturally conscious groups would discover once and again fresh identity symbols and identity artefacts in these 'archives', thereby breathing new life (inspiration) into their cultural practices.

Despite his concern that the whole process might lead to an uprooting, Arguedas never lost faith in the tenacity of the Andean cultures and their capacity to deal with wrenching new contexts. In his novels, he closely monitored social developments, exploring the ways in which indigenous communities themselves tried to cope with the new situations. We see, for example, that talented young Indians were sent by the community[11] elders to the big city in order to gain 'Western' knowledge, sometimes for such a concrete purpose as the construction of a road leading to the big cities. His literary productions show Arguedas as an author who dreams indigenously, at times evoking in a poetical way the intense indigenous experience of nature, elsewhere predicting the historical uprisings of the 'comuneros' in the 1960s. His greatest literary concern was to translate indigenous oral culture into the dominant written culture he had managed to master so well. This obsession runs throughout his entire *oeuvre* and culminated in his masterwork, which was also his farewell novel: *El zorro de arriba y el zorro de abajo* (Arguedas 1988, orig. 1969). This book became a truly 'avant-garde' fresco of the ways of life of shattered but not completely uprooted Indian migrants, as well as of some desperate *criollos* and *gringos*, in a large industrial coastal town (Chimbote).[12] Extremely personal diary fragments and mythological dialogues between two foxes about the actual situation in Perú and the world served as a counterpoint to this fresco. It was Arguedas's way of exploring the obscure roads the Andean traditions would have to follow in the capitalist and transnational contexts of the big cities of which he was so apprehensive.

Arguedas's thinking in general has been much appreciated by the Latin-American and Spanish intelligentsia. His work has been the object of frequent colloquia.[13] His continued relevance has to do with the fact that he stubbornly kept raising the question about the survival of an Andean and 'Indo-American' pattern of identities. This remains a valuable approach because in the current international state of affairs, countries like Bolivia and Peru threaten to succumb as weak and insignificant 'little brothers'. As a scientist and as an artist, Arguedas managed to create a work that made it possible to both dream and think pragmatically about the inevitable socio-cultural transformations in the Andes.

Arguedas's integrity is impressive, even though his former admirer, Mario Vargas Llosa, recently disposed of his thinking as an 'archaic utopia'. Vargas Llosa (1997), in what is nonetheless an understanding and interesting study about Arguedas and *indigenismo*, calls his fellow writer a conservative 'cultural ecologist'.[14] Terms like 'utopia' and 'cultural conservationism' are always available when reference is made to people who are positively disposed towards the future of the indigenous cultures. This disposition cannot be conflated with the idea of sacred social and 'civilisational' progress. Critical exceptions are the essays of Peruvian historian Alberto Flores Galindo, published in his *Identidad y Utopía en los Andes* (1986). In an earlier study (De Munter 1994) we observed that, in the specific case of Perú, Arguedas's principle of hope and the indigenous population itself suffered enormously after the writer's death in 1969. First, this was the case with the failed land reforms by the leftist military regime, then, with the horrible social and cultural destruction resulting from the combination of Sendero Luminoso's blind terrorism and the merciless conduct of the army, and, finally, during Fujimori's pernicious regime. Still more people fled to the megalopolis Lima, joining the already massive throng of Andean migrants. In the final chapter of his study, Vargas Llosa rightly refers to this situation. In his view, it is the final *coup de grâce* to the indigenous utopia; from now on, the indigenous groups are condemned to a process of becoming increasingly desperate and uprooted (*desindianización*). However, he loses sight of the fact that in the second half of the 1990s, a comeback movement began to return these traumatised people to their homelands. Admittedly, most will stay in Lima, but, according to several authors, that is precisely where a complex process of cultural 'Andinisation' is taking place (e.g., Adams and Golte 1990). Vargas Llosa underestimates the effective energy of roots, cultural intuitions and their resulting practices. In the case of Lima, he too mentions the 'newly' born chicha-culture and the informal circuits that are created in such powerful ways.

Radical indigenous organisations nowadays look at Arguedas's theories from yet another critical perspective: to them, he is a white and thus unreliable mestizo (note Arguedas's completely different conception of *indigenous mestizos* as possible saviours of the tradition), whereas the only good thinking can but come from within. For the radical Aymara in Bolivia, for instance, where the indigenous people still constitute at least one-third of the total population, until recently the radical, sometimes even racist, anti-white writings of Fausto Reynaga were the bible of unbending indigenous identity and Marxist struggle for freedom. In 2003, the new kind of coalition arising between indigenous and syndicalist movements around the charismatic leader *El Mallku* Felipe Quispe and the Aymara deputy and defender of the *cocaleros* Evo Morales, seems to represent a very important popular force of opposition in Bolivia, even though it may evolve discordantly.

As always, the situation is more complex than some might want to have us believe. Well-meaning thinkers such as Arguedas conceived modern indigenous mestizaje as a survival strategy for the native cultures. Others find in this vision the same drive to assimilation that characterises the destructive and homogenising politics of the official regimes.

In any event, Arguedas warned at a very early stage that the 'indigenous problem' would not be solved through, nor could be reduced to, the creation of a kind of folkloric reservation (as official politics tend to do) or authentic relic (as culturalists might defend). The whole issue was about living traditions with the right to adopt – and adapt – 'strange' elements from another group. In his opinion, there was a 'monstrous misunderstanding' about this historical interaction with the hegemonic 'white' Latin-American culture. Dichotomist dilemma-thinking – Western versus native; universal versus particular; hegemonic versus oppressed, etc. – was not a useful way of approaching new, intense and very complex social changes. The ability to adopt, communicate and transform other cultural practices can accord perfectly with the idea of continuity qua tradition. Ticio Escobar, the lucid Paraguayan anthropologist and art historian, applies this conviction to the field of 'art' (Escobar 1993: 34):

> A certain ethnocentric stance, which is deeply embedded in cultural criticism, tends to think that only the forms of erudite art have a right to renew themselves and to change, whereas those of indigenous art, as is the case for popular art in general, are condemned to remain eternally virgin, identical to themselves and uncontaminated by history. When reference is made to modern art, it always, albeit implicitly, concerns enlightened art. Nobody would dream of mentioning modernity or studying the processes of historical development of indigenous creation. And if it is admitted that indigenous art undergoes stylistic or technical changes, such admissions convey rebuke and sorrow, hence always a negative attitude.

The right to change is denied to other cultures.

Actual Theories on Latin-American 'Identities'

In this section, I would like to comment briefly on the work of two important Latin-American social scientists who have been working from different angles on the question of identity processes in a globalising modernity. I do not aim to discuss exhaustively their general theoretical points of view, but it may be interesting to present their complementary points of view in order to provide a relevant idea of how this complex subject matter is being approached in Latin America. One of the approaches, defended by Jorge Larraín Ibáñez, is more universal and broadly Latin-American (overlooking 'the Indian'); the other, advocated by Néstor García Canclini, refers more concretely to the new game between consumers and global supply in the context of the megalopolis (with a certain attention to native versions and practices), which relates his work in an interesting way to the late Arguedas.

Modernidad, Razón e Identidad en América Latina (Modernity, Reason and Identity in Latin America) is the emblematic title of the book published in 1996 by the Chilean sociologist Jorge Larraín Ibáñez. Larraín is known for his work at the Department of Cultural Studies at Birmingham University, and has collaborated with ILADES, the well-known Latin-American research centre for the social sciences. The aforementioned book was first published in Chile, the author's native country, as something like a grateful return to the cultural puzzle of the continent where he grew up. It shows an admirable commitment against any form of thinking which reifies culture. Despite, or perhaps precisely because of the author's anti essentialist convictions, this intelligent book contains almost no reflection about or even understanding of the contributions which could be made by native cultural traditions in the actual societal context, which, according to Larraín, was fundamentally distorted by instrumental reason. With his Chilean background – Larraín was educated in theology and sociology at the rather conservative Pontificia Universidad Católica de Chile – he seems to have had little or no empathy with indigenous meanings.

The author elaborates a critique of the evolution of Latin-American identity, from the Conquista until today. The priority he gives to Latin-American identity in general, even when stressing the evident intertwining with the different national, regional and individual identities, is typical of this sociologist, who still believes in a universal applicability of the modern project. He argues that even if this project does not attain completion (and even less in the often 'indecent' social conditions of the Americas), it should nonetheless have its emancipatory chances, albeit it in constantly renewed ways. This is why he fiercely opposes currently fashionable essentialist and 'postmodern' positions,[15] which he characterises as 'simplifying tendencies that suppose the existence of a unique and definitive cultural essence or matrix' (Laraín 1996: 14). This is also why he dedicates the second part of his book to unravelling different forms and dimensions of essentialism – some subtle, some less so – in the thinking about national and personal identities on his continent. Larraín Ibáñez divides them into two large groups: on the one hand, essentialisms that stress the importance of a certain ethnic or cultural factor and reject the hybrid; on the other, those that accept 'mestizaje' but deny its ongoing evolution. The author especially scrutinises this last kind of discourse (ideology), with its more hidden essentialism. In this context, he explicitly criticises, amongst others, Chilean sociologist Pedro Morandé's theory about a unifying popular religiosity and Mexican Octavio Paz's 'latent nostalgia for the true identity'.[16]

It would be a mistake to view Larraín simply as an obsolete defender of modernity who puts the universal above the particular, thereby endorsing in his own way a kind of overarching mestizaje (over and against local or indigenous particularisms), for he endeavours to criticise precisely this superficial, general image. The existence of an all-encompassing Latin-American identity (with its historically undeniable foundation: the Conquista, which gave rise to a common master language(s) and religion) has been constructed and construed in a pernicious, superficial version from outside, Europe to begin with. He shows, clearly being irritated by this, how, from the sixteenth century onwards, Europe, including important and appreciated thinkers such as Marx and Engels, discursively constructed 'South America' as an indistinctive whole, and almost always in a pejorative sense (cf. Said's *Orientalism*). Importantly, Europe needed this simplified labelling that was directed outwards in order to differentiate and develop its own internal identities. Precisely this 'othering', which reduced the heterogeneity of Latin America to a shallow, inferior whole, is an illustration of how reason – reduced to its instrumental dimension – leads to forms of racism. The postmodernist and historicist option on difference is criticised even more severely in this sense.

For Larraín, cultural identity is intimately entwined with personal identity. Culture is brought about by public discourses, on the one hand, and by the more implicit, 'everyday' ways of life, on the other. It consists of several categories (like nation, gender, class and religion), which are the most important factors in determining personal identities. Larraín refuses to accept certain postmodernist positions, with their view of the fragmentation of the socially dependent person, even though he recognises that globalisation can, in some cases, have a devastating impact. Instead of talking about a dislocated identity, Larraín prefers to speak about a continued obligation to consider the real living conditions and relationships with others, however radical the changes may be. Even if it were true that the importance of some of the formerly determining categories like nation and class has diminished; even if it were true that it has become more difficult for people to perceive continuity between past and present; even if it were true that a globalised media supply might seriously obstruct a better understanding of the other, even if all this were true,[17] we cannot accept losing the belief in the capacity of human beings to attempt to change their circumstances. Personal identities – and, we could add according to the introductory chapter to this volume, group and community identities – are never completely dissolved. Instead, they are constructed and defined over and over again within new cultural contexts. The emphasis in Larraín's work clearly falls on the 'makeability' of the world. This is why 'postmodernism' – reified in the article for the sake of the author's argument – is criticised as being a kind of philosophical support for the neo-liberal political dream, namely an ideological weapon that aims to convince people that it is impossible to act politically in society. Thus, postmodernism can be a dangerous ideology in what he views as a time of confusion and rapid change.

Larraín views postmodernist claims to the effect that people may change their identities as one changes clothes as an absolutist interpretation of real living conditions, that is, of people trying to determinate their lives, acting and being prevented from acting by very real, changing social contexts. The fading away of categories which determine identities, such as class and nation, coincides with the rise of other relevant social contexts (ethnic, sexual and others). With regard to the globalised context of the process of identity formation, he asserts – as is the case with most theories on globalisation – that universalising and particularising tendencies are intertwined in a mutual and complex relation.

Nonetheless, Larraín's emphasis on the homogenising power of globalisation, above what the variety of particular (regional, etc.) tendencies could achieve, is characteristic of his approach. As Canclini's analyses suggest, Larraín's approach is too massive in its opposition of particularisation and globalisation, which matches with mega-identities such as 'Latin-American' and 'mestizo'.

Up to a certain point this allows us to understand why Larraín proves to be less informed about the actual importance and interests of indigenous cultures and their representatives. As we have already remarked, he does not seem to be really interested in what they could possibly contribute to intercultural processes (see for instance Mignolo 2000 on 'border thinking'). Moreover, when he does mention indigenous cultures, he reduces them to historical clichés. He asserts, for instance, that they were economically, technologically and military underdeveloped, compared to the Spanish (European) culture. This view is all the more peculiar considering that in the author's homeland, Chile, the native Mapuche remained indomitable during several centuries. Larraín talks about the defeat of the indigenous groups (another ideology of *la visión de los vencidos*?) but does not mention the continuous political and cultural insurrections, from Taqi Onqoy to Chiapas, nor the recent political rise of indigenous movements in Ecuador and Bolivia. These uprisings continue to take place, despite the destruction of the historical forms of indigenous cultures, which the *lógica de la colonización* strove to obliterate. Larraín speaks about the fatalistic conception of history of indigenous cultures, whereas, in fact, this conception deserves to be called dynamic and cyclic, in the rich, spiral sense of the word. In short, Larraín views them as cultures for which the past lies ahead and the future behind. Seen from within their own cultural intuitions, this is indeed the case, but the interpretation of this subtle intuition should not be carried out from within our own conceptual framework.

Despite his simplistic picture of the role of indigenous groups (which he clearly does not want to re-present), and despite a political stance that sometimes approaches that of the enlightened 'criollos' at the beginning of the twentieth century, who viewed native cultures as an obstacle to – 'their' – modernity, Larraín has nevertheless succeeded in showing that most studies on Latin-American national identities emphasise public versions of identity whilst neglecting the private ones. On the one hand, he argues that a great deal of attention has been devoted to the explicit expressions of identity, as produced by all kinds of institutions (universities, mass media, etc.), to which 'ordinary people', as producers of culture, do not always have access. On the other, he asserts that insufficient attention has been paid to more implicit expressions of identity that arise in relatively enclosed environments, in the 'multiple conversations and exchanges of everyday life'.

This is precisely the point at which Larraín's Argentinian colleague, Néstor García Canclini, takes up the challenge. Canclini has worked in Mexico since 1976, originally within a Marxist- and Gramscian-orientated theoretical framework. His research displays a profound interest in what Larraín called 'implicit expressions' of identity (for instance, the production of handicrafts) and, more specifically, in their relation to mass media, cultural policy and consumption.

Whereas Larraín defends, in a somewhat decontextualised fashion, the capacity of an individual to act politically, Canclini examines the concrete, politico-cultural relation between what he calls *ciudadanía* (i.e., contextualized citizenship) and consumption, in the broad, cultural sense of the term. His publications usually rely on long-term team research in the field. As an anthropologist, Canclini advocates the research methods of his discipline, which include an eye for details and their relation to the whole. This is why he clearly eschews the all too massive dichotomy between globalisation and particularisation, seeking instead to understand how differences evolve and interact in changing social contexts, taking into account, amongst others, the interconnectedness between the global and the local.

Canclini looks more 'postmodernist' – in a good sense of the term, i.e., with attention to creativity as 'combination' through time, with an open analysis of the new media, etc. But perhaps most interesting are his valuable proposals to improve (cultural) policies in reply to an increasingly multicultural world. The indigenous presence in this complex game is taken into consideration, but only as an element of the complex urban field he usually writes about, Mexico City. This anthropological anchoring allows him to convincingly relate his theoretical thinking to everyday realities, hence to the implicit expressions of identity Larraín referred to.

The two books for which Canclini is best known are *Culturas híbridas. Estrategias para entrar y salir de la modernidad*, published in 1989, and *Consumidores y ciudadanos. Conflictos multiculturales de la globalización*, published in 1995. The former focuses specifically on the world of art, popular art, cultural policies and cultural consumption, in view of examining the relationship between modernity and identity. The second directly tackles the question that interests us in this essay. As an urban anthropologist of the megalopolis Mexico City, Canclini shows a particular interest in the impact of mass media on this city. Even though there are great variations with respect to the supply, equality and extension of consumption in the important cities of Latin America, all exhibit an apparently labyrinth-type crossover of very diverse material and symbolic artefacts and trajectories. The challenge of similarly 'chaotic' settings requires an interdisciplinary approach which avoids the unfortunate distinction favoured by specialists between 'high' culture, 'popular' culture and 'mass' culture. The author also denounces the fallacious model of identity as authenticity, connected with an indispensable combination of territory and heritage. Accordingly, Canclini takes issue with an essentialist conception of identity.

What makes Canclini's theoretical and empirical work so interesting is the fact that the constantly changing social world is taken seriously in all its dimensions (i.e., media, popular art, elitist art, ideology, oral stories, crafts and markets, etc.). This is why, for instance, there is no disapproval of the mediatised and popular supply of cultural artefacts. Canclini is of course aware of the fact that consumption, due to the neo-liberal motor of globalisation, does not evolve equitably. For most people, novelties are merely consumption items; for some, they are merely a spectacle. The right to be a citizen, which in its fullest sense would also include deciding on how and when to produce, distribute and use commodities, is, as always, apparently limited to the elites. Nevertheless, Canclini would strongly agree with the central insight of Mary Douglas and Baron Isherwood's (1979) 'anthropology of consumption': commodities serve to make people think. According to Canclini, people think and choose when they consume, they reelaborate social meanings. 'Consumption' contains far more active forms of participation than the word would seem to imply at first sight. These processes of 'productive consumption' – in the case of native cultures especially concerning the crafts and the ways they organise and conceive their 'markets'[18] – inspire Canclini in his quest for new and better forms of citizenship. He observes, in this context, that, for a long time, the world of leftist thinkers has been cursed with what he calls a 'Gutemberghian cultural policy'. The parallel existence of 'popular cultures' that forms a kind of 'plebeian public sphere', informal and organised via oral and visual communication, has been recognised only slowly (Bakhtin, Gramsci, Williams, Hoggart). Indigenous cultures provide a marvellous example in this respect, and certainly more than that. However, the theoretical appreciation of these 'circuits'[19] still needs to be developed.

The appearance of different information channels makes it possible to understand the communities to which one belongs, to conceive and to exercise the rights related to them. Disenchanted with multiple bureaucracies (state, party, union), the public turns to the radio and television in order to obtain what the so-called civil institutions do not offer, namely, services, information, some justice and, simply, attention. This is by no means to say that these media are more efficient than official organisms; but they fascinate because people feel that they are listened to and no paperwork is required. In general, these media seem transparent in comparison with the opacity of official venues. Naturally, the use of popular communication channels does not alter the fact that these channels are often involved in global profit-making and political power. Nevertheless, our own field research with urban natives in Bolivia shows that people are quite aware of the ideological orientation of what they are looking at or listening to.[20]

García Canclini shows how the participation in transnational and uprooted consumer communities increasingly redefines identity in the large Latin-American cities. He also notes, with regard to the possible evolution of citizenship, a transition from the citizen as a representative of 'public opinion' towards the citizen as a consumer interested in a certain quality of life. Canclini obviously realises that civil society and citizenship have lately become concepts which are as totalising as was the case for 'the people' or 'the popular'; these terms are all meant to deny the heterogeneity of voices within the concerned countries. To avoid this kind of ideology, Canclini continues to distinguish between different spheres in civil society: the intimate sphere of (extended) family, the sphere of voluntary associations, the sphere of social movements and the different modes of public communication. Focusing on the last of these spheres, Canclini asserts that the classical definition of identity based on territory and social group must be complemented by a socio-communicational definition thereof, also transnationally, i.e., taking into account how identities evolve following new, complex ways of mass communication, 'co-production' and consumption. The poignant question then becomes which kind of identitary policy or which kind of citizenship could best suit these new kinds of identities. Bearing the former in mind, it would also be interesting to consider the different dimensions of temporality in order to elaborate a more open, flexible approximation to identity processes.

More than ever, 'losing one's identity' has become a nonsensical expression. Globalisation can have various effects, as it is always intertwined with strong modes of localisation. Additionally, the view that consumers would behave in irrational ways is facile. Canclini mentions the interesting anthropological example of the redistributing potlatch, sporadic tremendous 'wasting' – in a Western economic perception – of 'surplus' during community feasts. Different expressions of this potlatch principle can still be found among the native population in the modern urban areas. Our fieldwork with the urban Aymara in Bolivia from 1995 to 1999 revealed intriguing illustrations of similar ways of economic behaviour, in the broadest cultural sense of this term. Consider, for example, the 'Aymara capitalists', rich merchants that live in La Paz. These merchants prefer to continue living in popular neighbourhoods of the city, where they feel at home. They spend huge amounts of money in funding important celebrations in these neighbourhoods, thereby taking on responsibility for these public feasts. More generally, most traditional Aymara who live in El Alto, La Paz's indigenous sister city, still practise *ayni*, a continuously updated, though simplified, version of the former, highly complex reciprocity system which was and still is fundamental to the functioning of the Aymara community – in the *comunidades* as well as in the city. This obliges them to sometimes spend almost all their earnings, or even to indebt themselves.[21] A taxi driver in La Paz once told me: 'What do you expect from these people, sir? They squander everything they earn when the first party comes around.' Any 'sensible' Western person would not understand this kind of behaviour, but, as Canclini observes for the case of Mexico, what matters is, apart from a possible 'religious' justification of big spending, the fact that it allows the cultural group to consecrate other rationalities, other ways of organising society – mostly along the sociality dimension, in which prestige, redistribution and honour (the spiralling way of sharing authority, in the case of the Aymara) play an important role. Or, looked at in the broader scope of consumption, as Canclini (1995: 49) himself puts it:

> I have observed among the indigenous groups in Mexico that the introduction of external – modern – objects is only accepted when these can be assimilated within the logic of the community. The growth in income, the increase and variety of the market's supply and the technical capacity to become familiarised with the new items and messages thanks to a higher degree of education, are not enough for the members of a group to simply throw themselves at these novelties. The desire to possess 'the new' does not appear to be something irrational or independent of the collective culture to which one belongs.[22]

The same can be said about the supply of so-called 'high culture' – theatre, opera, expositions and the like. If people do not respond to this kind of supply, this is not merely due to an insufficient symbolic background, but also and primarily because of their allegiance to the groups they belong to. These groups restructure themselves and, in this heterogeneous flux, people continue to find codes that bring them together, that allow them to communicate. According to Canclini, these shared codes are less and less those of the ethnic group, class or nation in which we are born. To the extent that these old elements survive, they are refor- mulated as 'mobile pacts for the lecture of the commodities and the messages'.

Canclini's contribution to the understanding of contemporary cultural dynamics is valuable, but perhaps he focuses too exclusively, for the sake of his theoretical framework, on identification processes through consumption (although he has also studied native and 'popular' production). In El Alto, for instance, the chance that citizenship and consumerism can enter a reasonable alliance seems rather limited, given the material poverty, the numbing working hours and, above all, the deficient political institutions. Nevertheless, it is a joy to see how people trade, compare, exchange and bargain (both material and symbolic goods). Radios and, if possible, small televisions are important com- panions in everyday life. During the long trip to work, individuals evaluate, complain, hope or reflect in silence. In order to fully appreciate these concrete ways of citizenship, factors other than merely consumption must be considered. Take, for example, the productive energy and ingenuity emanating from the informal sector or the intense relations with the rural communities of origin.

Canclini's analysis is flexible enough to take all these local and cultural fac- tors – also 'time' – into account, even though he subordinates them to his gen- eral paradigm of how people engage in new modes of consumption and 'co-production'. Nevertheless, George Yúdice, in his excellent 2001 introduc- tion to García Canclini's work, with a profound and comprehensive approxi- mation of Canclini's non voluntarist attitude vis-à-vis the so-called subaltern, remarks appropriately that 'Canclini does not go far enough in his critique of the situation of blacks and Indians who have less leeway in negotiating away from the stigma of race... [in Latin America] "unmixed" blacks and Indians are generally excluded' (Yúdice in Canclini 2001: xxxvii). When Canclini is emphasising the relative plasticity of (crossing) identities in Latin-American contexts – in contrast to what happens, according to him, in the United States – it seems to me that he is accepting somehow, and maybe unwillingly, the nor- mality (not normativity) of a general, overriding mestizo identity.

In any case, García Canclini approaches modes of 'consumption' in a pro- found and culturally contextualised manner. Moreover, Canclini couples sci- entific research about the interaction and communication of a variety of cultural groups in Latin America with a pragmatic quest for alternative cultural policies: '... his Latin-American cultural space would be a preferable alternative to national cultural policies that have reified folkloric or high-art norms' (ibid. xxxviii).

'One must walk like a people':[23] Creative Identity-formation Among the Aymara in Bolivia

Hitherto we have discussed Latin-American identity processes in general terms, together with the manner in which these processes could be intertwined with indigenous progression. It would now be interesting to relate aspects discussed by authors such as Arguedas and Canclini to the complex historical evolution and no less complex current situation of the Aymara, and to Bolivia, the nation state in which the majority of this indigenous group live. This analysis is part of a broader inquiry[24] in which we attempt, on the one hand, to offer a multi-layered ethnographic perspective of the cultural dynamics in which the Aymara are engaged and, on the other, to develop a critique of the anthropological literature on this subject (reducing the lived presence of the people in a variety of ways, structuralist, subaltern, etc.). Accordingly, this section can only briefly illustrate the intriguing case of the progression of a contemporary indigenous group, embedded in a modern, globalising context. While the social situation in contemporary Bolivia still contains colonial features (Rivera Cusicanqui 1993), there are important signs of growing and inspiring indigenous consciousness and resistance. Although this situation is not comparable to the way in which they 'walked' some five hundred years ago, they are still 'walking like jaqi': the Aymara people.

The Bolivian Aymara, who comprise more than 1.5 million of a total population of approximately 7.5 million inhabitants, live in a land that once was one of the four regions composing *Tawantinsuyu*, the vast empire of the Incas, the culture which spoke the Quechua language and which governed at the time of the Spanish invasion. The Aymaras, however, associate themselves with the cultural horizon of *Tiwanaku*, a culture which flourished several centuries before the Incas.

The indigenous heart of Bolivia is principally located in the Andean highlands. Whereas the Quechua, faithful to their traditions, remained in the more fertile valleys, the Aymara engaged in an impressive interaction with their majestic but harsh habitat, the Altiplano, situated at an altitude of 4000 metres, and which gradually rises from Lake Titicaca to the sacred summits of the Andes. Behind the summits lie subtropical valleys. La Paz, the capital of Bolivia, lies at an eastern extremity of the Altiplano, in a valley that is almost completely urbanized. Contiguous to or more precisely above La Paz, lies its sister city, El Alto, which has, as mentioned before, witnessed an exponential growth quite literally at the edge of the Altiplano. Founded originally around some *comunidades originarias* – the first, indigenous communities – El Alto has grown continuously and now has some 700,000 inhabitants. The majority of its inhabitants come from the impoverished Aymara countryside; another important group are Quechua migrants, mostly relatives of the families of mineworkers that ended up in El Alto after the brutal closing of the state-owned mines in 1985.

Anthropologically speaking, El Alto is a fascinating anthill, composed of indeterminately articulated neighbourhoods that usually assemble people from a common region and who live in great poverty. Nonetheless, the city exudes vitality. Intense and culturally differentiated trading takes place everywhere. People get together to celebrate or simply for neighbourhood meetings. Many spend part of their time farming, sometimes in their back garden – including the cultivation of the famous deepfreeze potatoes called *ch'uñus* – usually in their *comunidades de origen*. The great majority of these rural migrants commute, when possible, to their villages to participate in ritual farming festivities or to bring back crops to El Alto. Conversely, they take with them agricultural products and gifts for family members who have remained in the rural community to tend to the crops. These are all manifestations of *ayni*, the fundamental principle of reciprocity.

The picture becomes more fascinating – and grimmer – when it includes La Paz. A veritable army of minibuses rushes down daily, filled with people who hope to earn some money in the richer, more modern lower city, or to have access to the means of education which are highly deficient in El Alto. They climb into these tightly packed minibuses in the numbing cold of the Altiplano dawns, at the behest of the *voceros* – literally 'shouters' – schoolboys who, hanging out of the door, cry out the names of the destinations and receive the payments. The ride brings them from the edge of the Altiplano to the centre of La Paz in half an hour. During this half hour of descent, they are confronted with the fascinating image of this patchwork puzzle that spreads out in piecemeal fashion across various altitudes. In effect, the ride stretches from the indigenous city on the Altiplano to the valley of La Paz. The latter's hills are culturally and demographically differentiated. One of the hills is where the Spaniards first settled, giving rise to the *criollo* city, La Paz. In front lies the hill populated by the *nouveau riche* Aymara, who determine the city's image. The higher (and colder) one climbs these hills, the poorer the dwellings. If one takes a second minibus yet further down, one reaches an altitude of some 3000 metres, which enjoys a far more hospitable climate. Here one finds residential neighbourhoods, nestled in a far more gentle landscape. This is where the rich classes live, as well as their indispensable – indigenous – housemaids; it is also where the embassies are located. In short, it is a world with a pronouncedly Western look.

Innumerable persons commute down to the valley, and although they naturally never really participate in this world, they nonetheless influence it and are influenced by it. There are thousands of women who take over the sidewalks with their wares and who, once installed, peer at everything; there are labourers, gardeners, and many others. They embody a large-scale and palpable contact with the other world, so deceptively portrayed in TV soap operas and advertisements. This is but one example of the numerous intercultural lines which are drawn, often full of misunderstandings and incomprehension. A painful example is the interaction between doctor and patient, which, in El Alto, can take place between a doctor from 'below', who has no idea of the cultural context in which his patient experiences and contextualises a disease, and an elderly Aymara like the above-mentioned don Casto, who has difficulty expressing her- or himself in Spanish. Sadly, such intercultural lines are usually a one-way traffic, both literally and figuratively. A sense of powerlessness, on the one hand, and a lack of understanding, on the other, characterise these encounters. Some racists stigmatise the Universidad Mayor de San Andrés in La Paz, which is the driving force of all kinds of social discussions, as the university of the *llamas*, because the majority of the students are of Aymara origin. Somewhat further down the valley one finds the Catholic elitist university for the children of the higher classes.

If we speak, within this intriguing sociogeographic picture, of creative identity-formation, this will refer almost exclusively to those who, having abandoned a relatively simple life in the countryside, with its rather rigid but tranquil lifestyle, are obliged to invent new forms of life in the multicultural double-city in view of rendering their (individual and group) identities more flexible, in order to keep on 'walking like jaqi', 'the (Aymara) people'. Gilberto Pauwels, a Flemish anthropologist who settled in Oruro thirty years ago and is an expert on the Aymara, shares this view. As he sees it, the Aymara culture will survive 'selectively', as a result of its contact with the urban culture. Although a great deal will be 'lost', the remaining elements will take on new forms and contents in a process of cultural creation, thereby enabling a continuous process of self-identification by the Aymara. An example is the *wiphala*, the radiant flag with a rainbow in a mosaic: although it was almost unknown twenty years ago, it has now become the uncontested symbol of the indigenous groups. The participants in this process are feverishly exploring other aspects of their cultural heritage, participating in new social interactions and, to a certain extent, engaging in the economic form of mestizaje which Arguedas held to be unavoidable.

Bolivian social scientists have been engaged in a protracted debate about changes in the indigenous groups and about mestizaje in the framework of contemporary Bolivian society. According to Rafael Archondo, there are three approaches to urban cultural mestizaje in Bolivia. The first views this mestizaje as a variety of the Andean original tradition; the second, as the decline of this tradition; the third, as an ethnogenesis, whereby urban life leads to a new mestizo identity (see the *chicha* culture, according to Vargas Llosa). Each of these approaches, which has been summarised here in a highly simplified form, is guilty of essentialist presuppositions concerning an authentic tradition, whether indigenous or mestizo.

The standpoints of the individual thinkers are obviously much more nuanced. Consider, in this context, the contribution of Silvia Rivera Cusicanqui. Her analysis of the Bolivian situation quickly chills the optimism of Larraín and Canclini, who believe in either a (Latin-American) reorientation of the project of modernity or in a resilient consumer as the driving force of a new kind of citizenship. She has doggedly studied the complex historical growth of the enduring bondage of the majority of the population, especially of the *indios* and the *cholos*. The cholos are the most ostentatiously urbanised of the indigenous people in Bolivia (the term often has a pejorative connotation, when this suits whoever uses it). Rivera Cusicanqui shows that in the course of the country's political evolution, beginning with liberal law-making in 1874 (which bestowed citizenship on the indios), then moving on to the National Revolution of 1952 (which recognised indigenous groups as landowners, albeit by grossly misunderstanding their community traditions)[25], and continuing up to the present political situation (including the labour unions), indigenous groups have been promised equality and rights only to the extent to which they renounced being Indio – Other – and took on the features of a Western citizen. In other words, rights and equality were subordinated to their becoming owners, commercial producers and consumers. Her perceptive analyses reveal enduring structures of domination which go hand in hand with the ongoing political exclusion of the majority and a continuous ethnic oppression. She thereby exposes the contradictions of the process of mestizaje, which brings together ideologically different temporalities (e.g., pre-Columbian, colonial, neo-liberal). This state of internal colonialism, Rivera Cusicanqui (1993: 123) asserts, constitutes 'perhaps the most structuring framework for the process of identity-formation. This state of affairs arises from a whole range of non-simultaneous contradictions between different cultural-civilisational horizons.'[26] Her description of what she rightly calls 'processes of cultural disciplining' and 'banishing the own culture into clandestineness' are unnerving, but, in our opinion, too fatalistic. She means the more structural forms of homogenising violence, such as coercion at school,[27] housemaid service, as well as the military service for young men, which not only includes direct indoctrination but also brute physical violence. Despite this sombre picture, Rivera Cusicanqui cherishes some hope about the resilience of the indigenous culture.

Other writers are more combative, but sometimes at the cost of naïve and idealistic exaggerations. Simón Yampara Huarachi, an Aymara, is an important advocate (and inventor) of indigenous traditions. He publishes regularly about the social organisation and community economics in the Andes. He too refers to internal colonialism and the antagonism between the two economic logics. But his main contribution has been to underscore the extent to which 'homogenising systems' have encountered resistance from the comunidades originarias and the Andean soul, which seem to survive, evergreen and intact, in his writings.

A positive feature of the current state of affairs is that there is a great deal of discussion at all levels. One may doubt, for example, whether government initiatives such as the *Participación Popular* of 1996 are viable translations, as some politicians assert, of Aymara proposals concerning participatory organisation and the reciprocity of traditional communities. But perhaps it points to a modest influence of the 'new citizens'.

A great deal of research still needs to be done concerning the concrete, everyday life of the indigenous groups engaged in the process of identity creation, and the ways in which they give meaning to their life. In the sphere of religious experience, for example, the Aymara rituals and religion have yet to be defeated,[28] as is shown by the enormous success of the offerings to Pachamama – 'the mother of time and space' – among large segments of the urban population, including families that have become less indigenous in their traditions. Undoubtedly, the manipulative and opportunistic interventions of various religious institutions have had a significant impact on Aymara religious experience. These numerous alternative religious movements take advantage of precarious living conditions, particularly of the fact that parents desire good and affordable schooling for their children.

Nevertheless, a slow evolution is perceptible in this domain. Although the so-called religious sects have been charged with 'culture destruction', there are unmistakable traces of a certain transformation whereby these sects have appropriated features of indigenous culture (see Prado Meza 1997). This is certainly the case for the popular Pentecost movement, which is being transformed from below in innumerable ways. In the course of my fieldwork, I have become acquainted with the *Catequistas* movement, which claims to be Catholic[29] and which enjoys a considerable number of followers in the indigenous rural neighbourhoods of El Alto. This movement comprises Aymara migrants who, without the aid of priest or shepherd, come together every week in an *uta* – a pivotal word in Aymara which means both dwelling and family – to sing in the Aymara language Christian songs which they have composed themselves. These songs evoke life in the countryside and are accompanied by autochthonous instruments. They also continue to celebrate the festivities of the agricultural calendar, and only the consumption of alcohol, so deeply rooted in the culture, is restricted. Intensive discussions about the problems of life in the large city take place at the margins of their large yearly get-togethers. Significantly, these meetings almost always take place in one or other sacred sites of the Altiplano, in accordance with Aymara traditions. This, again, is a good example of how a culture transforms itself in the midst of a new context.

As the majority of the urban indigenous people are entirely excluded from the social facilities available to the elites, they rely on and further develop endogenous networks. Other examples of ways of making urban life emergent and liveable include group music, the ayni (including the *compadrazgo* system, which is a vertical development of the more intimate extended family), and the use of traditional medicinal cures.

While playing music has traditionally been reserved for men, many women have devoted themselves to textile weaving, since time immemorial the artefact par excellence by which to express different identities in the Andes. It is the women in particular who have been the organic symbols of the group's continuity, yet forced to witness the decline of this rich tradition. Although a lot of weaving is still done, its quality is swiftly diminishing, as little time is available for it. Many young women who arrive from the countryside, where slings made of traditional, hand-woven fabrics are still used, switch over to cheap industrial versions of these fabrics, or simply abandon them altogether, for it is important to integrate into a work-environment and to avoid being laughed at. Others take pride in possessing a *cholita* wardrobe, which is the style of the newly urbanised indigenous woman, with expensive borsalino hats and richly embroidered capes. Historically speaking, this traditional costume arose as a mimesis of the white castes, yet this wardrobe has become a proud symbol of identity (despite the mockery of the white elites). See here an intriguing interaction between *ipséité* and *mêmeté*.

Despite their urbanised attire, the eyes of many of these women wax nostalgic when one speaks with them about meaning and praxis of the traditional textures. A happy few can work in cooperative ventures, where textiles made of dyed wool are produced for tourists or for export. On the other hand, the fact that the middle and high-middle classes continue to admire whatever comes from the West creates a thick mist which hampers understanding the possible meaning of evolving indigenous cultures. 'The Indian' is perhaps best off with the stubborn and self-assured patterns of progression which characterise the so-called poor and subaltern indigenous groups. As we suggest elsewhere extensively, these ways and rhythms of intersecting progression might be paced by cultural intuitions like 'contextualisation' and 'the sense of the plurivalence' vis-à-vis the elements of *pacha*, this is, in their conception, the broadest, all-embracing context of time and space. These cultural intuitions seem to guarantee as yet the cultural transmission, and do so mainly along the sociality dimension mentioned in the introductory text of this book.

Significantly, these patterns are also visible amongst the youth in El Alto. True, the young people have had periods of marked and sometimes radical opposition to traditional culture. During such times, they eagerly explore and play with Western cultural forms available in the city. But youngsters often end up returning to a traditional, yet vigorous culture.[30] They go ahead and reinterpret this culture, drawing on their other experiences, yet are intuitively convinced of the need to continue 'walking as (a) people'. This is probably the reason for which our main informant, Ricardo Mendoza Mamani, when reflecting about contemporary changes, was so concerned about maintaining the socialising dimension which characterises the Aymara. As he put it, 'hay que practicar la familia' – family must be practised. This idea is directly relevant to respect for the other and to the ubiquitous ayni, reciprocal help. These practices ensure that the Aymara continue to 'move on as (a) people'. And this guarantees, as he noted several times during our fieldwork, that the Aymara community, including El Alto, continues to be woven together, albeit in a broader, more diffuse manner.

A fascinating recent study[31] under the direction of Rafael Archondo has also confirmed the dynamic which characterises 'tide'-wise the culture of the youth in El Alto. Archondo works with a team of enthusiastic young researchers from El Alto. It is encouraging that the departments of social science and philosophy of the poor university of La Paz can count on the support of children of Aymara migrants, even though these children initially have difficulties in dealing with their identities as a result of the racism to which they have been subjected. These children are not stuffed up with the noncommittal theories that have reached them from the West. They study cultural processes in which they themselves are embedded. This is perhaps the reason why they are so fascinated by renewed ideas about indigenous reciprocity (Temple 1995). Little does it matter whether or not these ideas are indigenous or utopian, as long as they inspire and support these people.

The real contribution of 'Latin America' could, therefore, be a culturally anchored reflection on reciprocity and redistribution. This could lead to a real encounter, to a mutual gift. Félix Layme, an alert Aymara linguist and specialist in the Andean oral tradition, made the following remark at the end of a colloquium on the contemporary meaning of reciprocity: 'Estando en vida podemos hacer algo' ('We can still do something, as long as we live').

Notes

1. *Arauco tiene una pena, que no la puedo callar, son injusticias de siglos, que todos ven aplicar nadie le ha puesto remedio, pudiéndolo remediar, levántate Huenchullán'*. Violeta Parra was a famous Chilean songwriter. I would like to thank my friend Hans Lindahl of Tilburg University (The Netherlands) for his invaluable assistance in the translation and the rewriting of the original text. I also thank my wife Sandra Coppia Acuña for the conversations on indigenous textile art in the Andes.

2. See the beautiful testimony of Leandro Condori, recorded by Esteban Ticona, in the publication series by THOA (Taller de Historia Andina) in La Paz (Leandro Condori Chura and Esteban Ticona, *Kasikinakan Purirarunakan qillqiripa / El escribano de los caciques apoderados*, THOA, La Paz, 1992). Here and throughout this article, the English translations of the quotes from Spanish authors are my own (Koen De Munter).

3. The Dutch philosopher of culture Ton Lemaire (1986) did something similar in his beautiful book, *De Indiaan in ons bewustzijn* (The Indian in our consciousness). The title of this paper is an allusion to this intelligent reflection about the encounter between the West and the so-called 'New World'.

4. See Xavier Albó and Raúl Barrios (1993), *Violencias encubiertas en Bolivia*, on hidden structural violence in Bolivian everyday life.

5. Of course, the situation in each country is different. In Mexico, for instance, the indigenous people certainly have been more present in the arts, public discourses and so on. But there too they have basically been seen as an obstacle to the national project (they would first have to be Mexican and only afterwards and innocently indigenous).

6. Abstracting from their often impoverished economic conditions, indigenous groups do not have, culturally speaking, a clear status in government politics: are they on the 'right' way to assimilation? Or do they have the power of the awesome Other? The image of the fatalist Indian notwithstanding, there have been continuous indigenous uprisings against hegemonic groups. A case in point is blockades by campesinos in Bolivia in 2001.

7. My wife Sandra Coppia and I carried out fieldwork with the urban Aymara in El Alto (Bolivia) during the period 1995–99.

8. Interview with Carlos Fuentes in *El País, Babelia*, 3–10–1992: 'Las Culturas van a determinar el nuevo orden mundial'.

9. Some interesting thinking in this line has been undertaken by the Frenchman Dominique Temple (1995, 1997). His studies on reciprocity, starting from Mauss's *Essai sur le don*, assert, among other things, that we should consider the 'historical quid pro quo' between a culture based on exchange, on the one hand, and, on the other, the indigenous cultures, in which the gift was the axis around which social-economic life (prestige, redistribution) resolved. Even though Temple's work is often considered utopian or at least radical by many Western scientists and international cooperation workers, it has met with much success among indigenous thinkers of the Andes and Amazon region. He attempts to ground his theoretical thinking – inspired by the French philosopher Lupasco – on the concrete practices and concepts that come from the native experience itself (this is why he would reject the Marxist label 'collectivistic' used by Arguedas).

10. It is important to emphasise that Arguedas's concept of mestizo/mestizaje is both historical and combatively emancipatory. Accordingly, it has nothing to do with the passive, mystifying concept of the mestizaje ideologists. See also García Canclini's ideas on consumption and citizenship below.

11. In this paper, the term 'community' refers to the actual, rather small-scale social units of indigenous people in the Andes. They use the Spanish word *comunidad* (a community can function together with other *comunidades* in a larger *ayllu*). We are not referring to the more abstract sense of this word in English.

12. When writing this book, Arguedas made a series of interviews with the inhabitants of Chimbote. *El zorro de arriba y el zorro de abajo* was published posthumously for the first time in 1971.

13. E.g., *José María Arguedas viente años después: huellas y horizonte* 1969–1989, Universidad de San Marcos, Lima, 1991. Also a homage publication: *José María Arguedas. Vida y Obra*, Amaru

editores, Lima, 1991. A double theme issue was published in Spain, in 1992, dedicated to the meaning of Arguedas's *oeuvre: JMA: indigenismo y mestizaje cultural como crisis contemporánea/* supplement 31: *JMA: una recuperación indigenista del mundo peruano. Una perspectiva de la creación latinoamericana.*

14. Mario Vargas Llosa's vision is understandable as he offers a (psychological-cultural) reading of Arguedas's novels, paying scant attention to his – far less known – anthropological production. All in all, Vargas Llosa shows far more empathy in this book with the indigenous issue than in his literary production and political ideology.

15. Larrain (1996: 14) argues that postmodernism in Latin America eventually allied itself with certain essentials, anti-modern stances.

16. In Morandé's theory, 'the' cultural identity of Latin America was consituted in the sixteenth century in the framework of a 'baroque or symbolic-dramatical matrix', in opposition to European Enlightenment. From this perspective, the real cultural synthesis in Latin America can be found in popular religiosity, which he calls a 'reservation of cultural identity'. Larrain objects to such a reading, as it implies that everything happening after the independence would have to be considered as an alienation from that original identity (instrumental reason, for example, cannot be viewed as constitutive thereof). Larrain (1996: 207) argues the following with regard to Octavio Paz: 'These theories take their point of departure in the fct that reality is de-centred, not well integrated, as the result of colonisation, of the imposing of cultural transplants. But these realities are not accepted. What remains, then, is nostalgia for the integration of a totally structured identity. But is that really possible? Can we talk about a total cultural unity within a country?'

17. Canclini and many others would resist such simply dichotomist interpretations.

18. Cf. his 1995 book, *Transforming Modernity: Popular Culture in México.* Austin: University of Texas Press.

19. 'We have, however, done very little in the way of a theoretical appreciation of these popular circuits as fora which make it possible to develop networks of exchange of information, where citizenship can be learned in relation to the consumption of contemporary mass media, beyond easy idealisations of political and communicational populism' (Canclini 1995: 34).

20. As a matter of fact, this should not come as a surprise: one of the basic linguistic intuitions of the Aymara language is the obligation to indicate the source of information. This can be achieved by means of a simple suffix.

21. Interestingly, increasing numbers of Aymara try to negotiate the ancestral *ayni* obligations, because life in the city – for example the schooling of the children – imposes other ways of economic activity and earning. But they also do so because the field of *ayni* application expands constantly in the city. For example, some will become part of an evangelical sect, which are generally opposed to traditional customs. By advocating their adherence to a sect they can avoid *ayni* spending. Nevertheless, they will go on applying *ayni* for the closest family (and compadres) and on the occasion of important feasts in their home communities.

22. Canclini also refers to Arjun Appadurai, who states that even in fully modern situations, consumption is never something 'private, atomised and privatesed' but always something 'extremely social, correlative and active', only subordinated to a certain control by political elites.

23. The central guideline amongst the Aymara is summarised in the aphorism, 'Jaqjam sarnaqaña'/'Hay que andar como gente' (One must walk as (a) people). 'People', *jaqi* in Aymara, refers to the own cultural group.

24. See my PhD thesis: 'Inheems voortgaan in de Andes. Culturele getijden bij de hedendaagse, stedelijke Aymara in El Alto (Bolivia)' / 'Indigenous progression in the Andes. Cultural tides among the contemporary, urban Aymara in El Alto (Bolivia)', Ghent University, 2003.

25. Numerous (revolutionary) reforms, which at first glance were sympathetic to the campesino and opposed to the great landowners, failed to appreciate and even thwarted one of the foundations of the Andean culture, namely the rural sense of community and its opposite forms of organisations. It is symptomatic that public discourses substituted the term 'campesino' for that of 'Indio', only to deride the former. This effect was reinforced by the dictatorships of the 1960s and 1970s (which did not hesitate to enlist the support of the religious sects widely pre-

sent in the countryside). Nevertheless, the dictatorships did not succeed entirely, as has been evidenced by the studies of Rivera and THOA (Taller de Historia Oral Andina) about the traditional forms of *ayllu,* whih was able to survive in some regions.

26. Rivera Cusicanqui has recently argued that an important paternalistic factor (oppression of women, even within emancipative movements) is intertwined with the general colonisation pattern. This allows her to avoid a perspective that is too ethnically determined: 'It would certainly be helpful, in view of clarifying vital issues concerning our understanding of the phenomenon of identity in Bolivia, to discuss mestizaje as a hegemonic, ideological construct, both patriarchal and colonialist.' In: *Mestizajes: Ilusiones y Realidades,* MUSEF 1996, p. 59.

27. See Aurolyn Luyckx's *The Citizen Factory: Schooling and Cultural Production in Bolivia* (1999).

28. See Fernández Juárez's *El banquete Aymara. Mesas y yatiris* (1995) and *Entre la repugnancia y la seducción. Ofrendas complejas en los Andes del Sur* (1997).

29. Back in the 1960s the Catequistas were indeed promoted by the Catholic Church in order to reach more people in remote areas (cf. the African experience). In El Alto, however, these groups give the impression of having become a kind of alternative religious group in their own right.

30. Here, in my opinion, lies the unique character of El Alto: the youth can fall back on a deeply-rooted culture – think of the obligatory trips to the comunidades – that, however timidly, evolves in a majority position. The authors of the endogenous study about the youth culture in El Alto (see the following footnote) refer to a 'cultural matrix', which should be understood as a flexible womb, rather than a rigid framework, that continues to hold sway and order new contributions.

31. See *T'inkazos (Revista boliviana de ciencias sociales),* January 2000: *Ecografía de la juventud alteña. Nuevas conductas sociales con raíces aymaras.* This article was a provisional report of fieldwork by Germán Guaygua, Angela Riveros and Máximo Quisbert. In the same issue appeared Rafael Archondo's *Ser chango en El Alto. Entre el rock y los sikuris (existencias fronterizas),* which draws on the aforementioned article. At the end of 2000 PIEB published a more complete round-up of the study: *Ser joven en El Alto. Rupturas y continuidades en la tradición cultural.*

Bibliography

Adams, Norma and Golte, Jurgen. 1990. *Los Caballos de Troya de los Invasores. Estrategias Campesinas en la Conquista de la Gran Lima.* Lima: IEP.

Albó, Xavier and Barrios, Raúl (eds.) 1993. *Violencias encubiertas en Bolivia* (2 parts). La Paz: Cipca-Aruwiyiri.

Archondo, Rafael. 1991. *Compadres al micrófono. La resurrección metropolitana del Ayllu.* La Paz: Hisbol.

Arguedas, José María. 1976. *Formación de una Cultura Nacional Indoamericana* (edition by A. Rama). México: Siglo XXI.

————— 1988. *El zorro de arriba y el zorro de abajo.* Lima: Horizonte.

De Munter, Koen. 1994. 'Mestizajes. José María Arguedas: antropologie en literatuur'. Ghent University, MA thesis.

Douglas, Mary and Isherwood, Baron. 1979. *The World of Goods. Towards an Anthropology of Consumption.* New York: Basic Books

Escobar, Ticio. 1993. *La Belleza de los otros. Arte indígena del Paraguay.* Asunción: RP Ediciones.

Fernández Juárez, Gerardo. 1995. *El banquete Aymara. Mesas y Yatiris.* La Paz: Hisbol.

————— 1997. *Entre la repugnancia y la seducción. Ofrendas complejas en los Andes del Sur.* Cusco: CBC.

Flores Galindo, Alberto. 1986. *Buscando un Inca. Identidad y Utopía en los Andes*. Lima: Horizonte.

García Canclini, Néstor. 1989. *Culturas Híbridas. Estrategias para entrar y salir de la modernidad*. México: Grijalbo.

——— 1995a. *Consumidores y Ciudadanos. Conflictos multiculturales de la globalización*. México: Grijalbo.

——— 1995b. *Transforming Modernity. Popular Culture in México*. Austin: University of Texas Press.

——— 2001. *Consumers and Citizens: Globalization and Multicultural Conflicts* (introduction by George Yúdice). Minneapolis: University of Minnesota Press.

Guaygua, Germán, Quisbert, Máximo and Riveros, Angela. 2000. *Ser joven en El Alto. Rupturas y continuidades en la tradición cultural*. La Paz: PIEB.

Larraín Ibáñez, Jorge. 1996. *Modernidad, Razón e Identidad en América Latina*. Santiago de Chile: Andrés Bello.

Lemaire, Ton. 1986. *De Indiaan in ons bewustzijn. De ontmoeting van de oude met de nieuwe wereld*. Baarn: Ambo.

Luyckx, Aurolyn. 1999. *The Citizen Factory: Schooling and Cultural Reproduction in Bolivia*. New York: SUNY Press.

Manrique, Nelson. 1993. *El Universo Mental de la Conquista de América*. Lima: Desco.

Mignolo, Walter. 2000. *Local Histories/Global Designs: Coloniality, Subaltern Knowledges, and Border Thinking*. Princeton, NJ: Princeton University Press.

Museo Nacional de Etnografía y Folklore. 1996. *Seminario/Mestizaje. Ilusiones y Realidades*, ed. MUSEF, La Paz.

Prado Meza, Amelia. 1997. *Dios es evangelista, no?* La Paz: Plural Editores.

Rivera Cusicanqui, Silvia. 1993. 'La raíz: colonizadores y colonizados'. In *Violencias Encubiertas en Bolivia* (Vol. 1), ed. Javier Albó. La Paz: CIPCA-Aruwiyiri.

——— 1999. 'Aportaciones fragmentarias entorno a la Interculturalidad'. In *Encuentro México-Bolivia sobre Cultura, Identidad y Globalización*. La Paz: Uma Phajsi Editores.

Sánchez Ferlosio, Rafael. 1994. *Esas Yndias Equivocadas y Malditas. Comentarios a la historia*. Barcelona: Destino.

Subirats, Eduardo. 1994. *El Continente Vacío. La Conquista del Nuevo Mundo y la Conciencia Moderna*. México: Siglo XXI.

Temple, Dominique. 1995. *La dialéctica del don. Ensayo sobre la oikonomía de las comunidades indígenas*. La Paz: Hisbol.

——— 1997. *La Réciprocité et la Naissance des Valeurs Humaines*. Paris: l'Harmattan.

Todorov, Tzvetan. 1982. *La conquête de l'Amérique. La question de l'autre*. Paris: Seuil.

Uslar Prieto, Arturo. 1997. *La invención de América mestiza*. México: FCE.

Vargas Llosa, Mario. 1997. *La Utopía Arcaica. José María Arguedas y las Ficciones del Indigenismo*. México: Fondo de Cultura Económica.

Photograph by Reinhart Cosaert, Moskou 1994

4

'FLOW BETWEEN FACT AND FICTION': ANALYSIS OF IDENTITY DYNAMICS IN VISUAL REPRESENTATION

An van Dienderen

Introduction

The picture presented on page 116 is the 'original' print of the image reproduced on the cover. At this point in the fabrication of the volume, I have no idea as to what the impact of the mode of production on the photo might be. The decisions made by the editors, the graphic designer, the marketing team, and others are left in the 'interval' between the moment when I write and the moment when the reader perceives the book. In this interval decisions are taken, meaning will flow, and perceptions change. Yet I want to start this contribution by analysing the differences between both pictures, since it seems a reflective way to roughly take up some of the issues elaborated in what follows. I therefore invite the reader to compare and weigh the importance of the changes.

What attracted me in viewing the image was the immediate closeness of the conversation between the man and the woman: the daily sharing of some thoughts, the movement of the man's head towards the woman as a way to make their space more intimate. But on a closer look, I noticed that what is in focus is not this cosy gathering, for the faces of the people are somewhat vague; it is the background: the wall with the two torn advertisements, the window with the reflection of a strip light. It becomes clear that the space defined by this sharpness of focus is a public space. It might be a bus, a train, or an airport hall. What this image suggests, then, is a moment grasped and defined by the communal character of the space. The tension between the intimacy of the two, and the sharpness of the background, is what makes this picture interesting. Public spaces are generally laden with cultural meanings, where the identity construction of a community takes place. Even though in recent times the analysis might be slightly different, as public spaces seem more segmented and privatised than they were decades ago, there is still a sense of marking going on. This marking or labelling throws us immediately into the discussion with which Pinxten and Verstraete started this volume. Shall we perceive this image as typically Russian, as the advertisements seem to suggest? Can we treat this image as a vehicle that is filled with ideological issues? Seemingly, this image is apt to do so. With the advertisements written in Russian but representing the Statue of Liberty, one can embark on topics such as the Cold War, power relations and deterritorialisation.[1] One could suggest that the hats indicate a cold climate, thus referring to Russia. Obviously, this kind of argument is rather weak in trying to classify a cultural identity. One may also argue that the central position of the persons is a typically Western approach of depicting figural scenes. However, as the aforementioned authors argue, the culturality dimension is only one of the parameters in defining identity dynamics. In this case, the identity of the people photographed is not only marked by the supposedly Russian characters – that would be a reduction of the perception induced by the image. The narrative of public spaces also consistently marks the persons. The public space is recognisable by all who have experienced urban environments and this identification might start off a sociological analysis. Moreover, the psychological and gender traits of this image are familiar to the viewers: the performances expressed by this man and woman construct a space of conversation which is common and so will be recognisable to many.

The picture on the cover and the one next to this article differ, although the image in itself is the same. The mode of production has shifted the interpretation. Is this an important shift? Do these differences change the reading of the image? Of course they do: a colour that is added, a shift in composition, a blurring of sharpness, all change the perception of an image drastically. In this example, the difference between the two images is such that the one on the cover is reduced to a mere illustration. The image next to this article is a complex reading that can be started with the shift in focus of the lens, defining a communal space, which leads to a composite identity dynamics characterised by urban, cultural and psychological elements, among others. The image on the cover has lost this complexity because it is impossible to view this shift in focus. Due to the blurring of the print and the reduction in focus, the viewer cannot see that there is an interesting tension between the people and their environment. The identity represented in this image is mainly characterised by its 'Russianness', the cultural identity marker to which the complexity of the picture as a whole has been reduced.

The above analysis is an example of the impact of the mode of production on identity dynamics in visual representations. As Pinxten and Verstraete argue, identity construction is based on the interplay of narratives and labels within a certain sociocultural context. In this view, labels are fixed identity markers and narratives are constantly mobile through the dynamics caused by the intertwining of fact and fiction. This contribution complements their theory on identity dynamics, in dealing with the dense and rich relationship between the construction of identities and the influence of visual media, particularly documentaries. The construction of the self (of an individual, a group, a community) and the construction of selves in visual representations are highly interlaced.

Arjun Appadurai provides a solid ground for the examination of the impact of electronic media in relation to migration, deterritorialisation and 'self-making': 'The importance of media is not so much as direct sources of new images and scenarios for life possibilities but as semiotic diacritics of great power, which also inflect social contact with the metropolitan world facilitated by other channels' (Appadurai 1996: 53). In order to further scrutinise this tangible affiliation between identity dynamics and visual representation, I will explore the mode of production of documentaries as a site of critique. Most often the mode of production is not taken into account: what is shown is perceived as real, as factual. The question of how the footage is filmed and edited is usually not traceable in the documentary itself. My aim is to look for methodological strategies in documentary production in which the mode of production functions as a site where the viewer can question the identity dynamics produced in the film. To legitimate methodological perspectives it is necessary to scrutinise the image itself. This research starts from the inherent *underspecification* of the visual. I will first present two paradigms on this important aspect of the image in order to contextualise the analysis of documentary footage. Thereafter I will turn to some methodological strategies developed in the seminars on visual anthropology at Ghent University, which were organised by Rik Pinxten and myself.

One paradigm is offered by the relativists Nelson Goodman and Catherine Elgin (1988). These authors developed a challenging theory in which they differentiate symbolic systems: representational or pictorial, linguistic and notational systems (1988: 9). They offer a comparison between those systems based on semantic and syntactic qualities by which the open tokenness of images is established. Cognitive linguists Gilles Fauconnier and Mark Turner have conceived another paradigm. Their theory on 'mental spaces' (Fauconnier, Lakoff and Sweetser 1994, Fauconnier 1997, Fauconnier and Turner 1999) offers challenging perspectives which allow for analyses of documentary as a blend between mode of production, content and form on the one hand, and a blend between fact and fiction on the other.

The Underspecification of Visual Representation

> *I will explain how a focus on visuality as such is really the first step toward dismantling of the classic epistemological foundations of anthropology and ethnography.*
> Rey Chow, *Primitive Passions*, p. 179

At the heart of the discussion on how to think of a methodological framework for representing others in images, there are several epistemological assumptions waiting to be challenged. One is on anthropology. Urged by Appadurai's invitation to anthropology to open up to cultural studies,[2] a redefinition of the discipline in function of the relationship between the world and word is being proposed (Appadurai 1996: 51–52):

> ... *word* can encompass all forms of textualized expression and *world* can mean anything from the means of production and the organisation of life-worlds to the globalized relations of cultural reproduction discussed here. Cultural studies conceived this way could be the basis for a cosmopolitan (global? macro? translocal?) ethnography. ... What the new style of ethnography can do is to capture the impact of deterritorialization on the imaginative resources of lived, local experiences. Put another way, the task of ethnography now becomes the unravelling of a conundrum: what is the nature of locality as a lived experience in a globalized, deterritorialized world?

Visuals and electronic mass media provide possible links between the different states of locality. The rich potentiality and importance of visuals in the construction of the self, on the one hand, and the formation of sodalities through those media, on the other, are important challenges to anthropology (Appadurai 1996: 7). Moreover, these transformations confront anthropology with the limitations of its methodologies in relation to the 'world'. It is not only the 'word' that is fruitful in exploring human transactions. Other types of symbol systems should be methodologically explored. According to Sarah Pink (2001: 5):

> social sciences should, as Mac Dougall has suggested, 'develop alternative objectives and methodologies' ... rather than attaching the visual to existing methodological principles and analytical frames. This means abandoning the possibility of a purely objective social science and rejecting the idea that the written word is essentially a superior medium of ethnographic representation. While images should not necessarily replace words as the dominant mode of research or representation, they should be regarded as an equally meaningful element of ethnographic work.

The Relativistic Approach

Goodman and Elgin (1988: 4) support a relativistic approach to epistemology. According to these authors, epistemology comprises understanding or cognition in all of its modes – including perception, depiction, and emotion as well as description:

> The mind ... is actively engaged in perception just as it is in other modes of cognition. Moreover, things do not present themselves to us in any privileged vocabulary or system of categories. We have and use a variety of vocabularies and systems of categories that yield different ways in which things can be faithfully represented or described. Nothing about a domain favours one faithful characterization of its objects over others. To choose among them requires knowing how the several systems function. (Goodman and Elgin 1988: 6–7)

Important then is to compare the symbolic systems and to evaluate their differences. The authors argue that an object can be presented in different symbolic systems: representational or pictorial, linguistic and notational (ibid.: 9). Comparison between those systems is based on their semantic and syntactic qualities. An important difference between pictorial systems and linguistic systems is the alphabet: languages have an alphabet, pictorial systems do not. Linguistic signs spelt in the same way are syntactic equivalents. Pictorial elements, on the other hand, can be similar but cannot be considered as syntactic equivalents. Therefore languages are syntactically differentiated, representational systems are syntactically dense. As far as semantics go, both of the systems are dense: which means there are many ways offered by both systems to describe a certain object. Goodman and Elgin claim that these semantic and syntactic differences are important because they influence the manner in which the systems are producing an order (1988: 9–13). As languages are syntactically differentiated, the exact repetition of articulation and inscription is possible. Representational systems are syntactically and semantically dense. A pictorial representation of an object can refine infinitely but loses a strict and precise description. There is no such thing as a visual alphabet to allow for the exact comparison of units. An image can therefore be described as an open token, a text cannot. The underspecification of visual representation is thus at the core of its characteristics:

> It is worth emphasizing that there is no single or 'correct' answer to the question, 'What does this image mean?' or 'What is this ad saying?' Since there is no law which can guarantee that things will have 'one, true meaning', or that meanings won't change over time, work in this area is bound to be interpretative – a debate between, not who is 'right' and who is 'wrong', but between equally plausible, though sometimes competing and contesting, meanings and interpretations. The best way to 'settle' such contested readings is to look again at the concrete example and try to justify one's 'reading' in detail in relation to the actual practices and forms of signification used, and what meanings they seem to you to be producing. (Stuart Hall in Rose 2001: 2)

Blending Fields

> Blends allow very generally for what Talmy (1995) calls *fictive* constructions, which are cognitively efficient because they remain linked to the relevant input spaces, so that inferences, emotions, and such can be transferred back and forth. 'Fictivity' is a crucial component of cognition and shapes everyday thought – scientific and artistic alike. (Fauconnier 1997: 164)

Gilles Fauconnier, George Lakoff, Eve Sweetser and Mark Turner have developed a theory of language from a cognitive point of view. This view is embedded in empirical experiments and investigates the evidence for basic mental operations that underlie language and which are indispensable to human understanding. It therefore goes 'beyond both a philological interest in the history of words and a formal interest in the patterns of grammar' (Fauconnier and Turner 1999: 416). In comparison with linguistic research, where the focus is on the structure of the signal itself (the language), they perceive language data as a way to access the nonlinguistic constructions to which the signal is connected (Fauconnier 1997: 4). The aim is to research the rich meaning constructions upon which language operates. The science of language they present breaks away from a type of research centred exclusively on syntax and phonology, and instead concentrates on analysing meaning construction. The latter 'refers to the high-level, complex mental operations that apply within and across domains when we think, act or communicate. The domains are also mental and they include background cognitive and conceptual models, as well as locally introduced mental spaces, which have only partial structure' (Fauconnier 1997: 1). Instead of assuming a priori and everyday-life conceptions of how human beings reason, talk and interact, this approach takes into account cultural and situational data as well as computational and biological evidence, in view of discovering some of the models, principles of organisation, and biological mechanisms that may be at work.

'Language, as we know it, is a superficial manifestation of hidden, highly abstract, cognitive constructions. Essential to such construction is the operation of structure projections between domains' (Fauconnier 1997: 34). One of these structure projections is mapping. In the most general mathematical sense of the term, mapping refers to defining a correspondence between two sets by assigning to each element in the first, a counterpart in the second (ibid.: 1). 'There has been mounting evidence for the central role played by various kinds of mapping at the very heart of natural language semantics and everyday reasoning' (Ibid.: 8–9). Other cognitive operations are analogy, metaphor, mental modelling, categorisation, framing and conceptual blending.

'Essential to the understanding of cognitive construction is the characterization of the domains over which projection takes place. Mental spaces are the domains that discourse builds up to provide a cognitive substrate for reasoning and for interfacing with the world' (Fauconnier 1997: 34). Mental spaces (Fauconnier, Lakoff and Sweetser 1994) are partial structures that proliferate when we think and talk, allowing for a fine-grained partitioning of our discourse and knowledge structure (Fauconnier 1997: 11). Mappings link mental spaces in several ways to construct meaning.[3] However, a description may originate in many mental spaces. Therefore a given sentence does not have a fixed set of readings; rather, it has a generative potential for producing a set of interpretations with respect to any discourse mental-space configuration (ibid.: 58). Moreover, 'The multiple possibilities do not stem from structural or logical ambiguities of the *language form*; they stem from its *space-building potential*: The language form contains *underspecified* instructions for space building' (Fauconnier 1997: 65; italics in the original). Thus, mental-space constructions generally deal with a considerable amount of underspecification in the process of meaning construction. There are no precise indications of properties; they are negotiable in further elaborations of the conversation (ibid.: 159).

Meaning can also be constructed through conceptual blending. 'Blending is in principle a simple operation, but in practice gives rise to myriad possibilities. It operates in two input mental spaces to yield a third space, the *blend*. The blend *inherits partial structure* from the input spaces and has *emergent structure* of its own' (Fauconnier 1997: 149). 'It plays a role in grammar, semantics, discourse, meaning, visual representation, mathematics, jokes, cartoons, and poetry. It is indispensable to the poetics of literature because it is fundamental to the poetics of mind' (Fauconnier and Turner 1999: 417). Blending is not restricted to language. It is common in visual representation, where it evokes conceptual blends (Fauconnier and Turner 1999: 406). Visuals in this approach are thus considered data, such as language evidence, in order to analyse the nonlinguistic constructions to which the signal is connected. As Shweta Narayan (2000: 47) notes in her study on conceptual mappings in *The Sandman* of Neil Gaiman: 'Again, this Case Study shows that visual manipulation of conceptual mappings in Comics is extremely sophisticated. It involves methods of evoking frames and creating mappings that cannot be exploited to the same extent in spoken language, and can therefore tell us something about conceptual mappings that language cannot reveal.'

Challenging about this is that the authors provide us with a theory on how to ground blended spaces. As Narayan remarks, in a genre like comics, different spaces within the representation can be blended to form a space which exceeds the meaning construction of the separate spaces: 'The three types of linguistic input (narrative boxes, speech bubbles and sound effects) are, therefore, blended with the visual space...' (Narayan 2000: 23). In this sense, the question is not whether there exists a hierarchy between words and images, but how the mind forms conceptual blends to construct meaning through several mental spaces induced by different data, and what this meaning construction might signify in the 'real' world. This view on the underspecification and the space-building potential of both words and images offers a refreshing challenge to the discussion. Throughout this article I will present some concrete examples of how this theory can be applied in the analysis of visual representation.

The Mode of Production as a Site of Critique

Analysis of Documentary Images

In view of these observations, it would prove interesting to analyse the use of documentary images. How do documentary filmmakers, television makers and the audience treat this underspecification of the image? And what is the significance of exploring the mode of production in this context?

Flow Between Fact and Fiction

> Inevitably, the distinction between fact and fiction blurs when claims about reality get cast as narratives. We enter a zone where the world put before us lies between one not our own and one that very well might be, between a world we may recognize as a fragment of our own and one that may seem fabricated from such fragments, between indexical (authentic) signs of reality and cinematic (invented) interpretations of this reality. (I use *indexical* to refer to signs that bear a physical trace of what they refer to, such as fingerprint, X ray, or photograph). (Nichols 1994: ix)

Documentary images are imbedded in an intangible relationship between the real and the imaginary. The mode of production is most often omitted. In this sense, the reconstruction of the real (this fiction) is perceived as fact. A deeply rooted confusion exists between the presented and the experienced reality, which blurs the urge for scrutiny. Because of the referential or indexical quality, images are wrongly taken for reality and, therefore, the production or constructionist level that is located between the experienced reality and the representation is neglected. The mode of production that allows for a representation of the reality is not taken into account because of the referential interpretation of images. As a result, the analysis of the process of identification in the visual system is much more complex than it appears at first sight. Conceptual blending offers an explanation for perceiving represented or filmed reality as the real: the content of those images is frame-blended with the form whereby the form only induces the cognition of the 'real', whether or not the form is actually factual. The typical documentary techniques are then blended with their 'original' content, which is claiming to reveal reality 'as it really happened'.[4]

> The very authenticity of the image testifies to the use of source material from the present moment, not the past. This presents the threat of disembodiment: the camera records those we see on screen with indexical fidelity, but these figures are also ghosts or simulacra of others who have already acted out their past. (Nichols 1994: 4)[5]

I used a super8 camera in my film *Visitors of the Night* (1998) to illustrate the reactions of the Mosuopeople in China on my digital camera. The super8 images can therefore be presented as more 'real', more authentic in relation to the mode of production of this film as they evoke the scene of filmmaking. However, the medium itself (super8) can work as an imaginary process, evoking memories of the early 1970s when it was used to produce home movies. The super8 images filmed on location in China projected this nostalgic remembrance of (Western) time past. The complexity thus created reveals an approach to the real in a multilayered way. It refuses to perceive reality as a good–bad fiction. 'A documentary aware of its own artifice is one that remains sensitive to the flow between fact and fiction' (Trinh 1990: 89).

Reconstruction Through Narratives

> [Narrative] is a means of symbolizing events without which their historicality cannot be indicated... because historicality itself is both a reality and a mystery. All narratives display this mystery and at the same time foreclose any inclination to despair over the failure to solve it by revealing what might be called its form in 'plot' and its content in the meaning with which the plot endows what would otherwise be mere event. Insofar as events and their aspects can be 'explained' by the methods of the sciences, they are, it would seem, thereby shown to be neither mysterious nor particularly historical. What can be explained about historical events is precisely what constitutes their non- or ahistorical aspect. What remains after events have been explained is both historical and meaningful insofar as it can be understood. And this remainder is understandable insofar as it can be 'grasped' in a symbolization, that is, shown to have the kind of meaning with which plots endow stories. (Hayden White, cited in Nichols 1994: 3)

In textual forms methodologies of critiques are inscribed within. Self-reflective methods, a bibliographical list, footnotes etc. are developed to present to the

reader a frame of reference in order to be able to judge the work. The accountability of the scientist can be located through these different strategies. In visual
systems of representation, those critical forms are lacking. A subject filmed does
not have a forum to question the standpoint of the director. The viewer is not initiated in the mode of production. There is no space within a visual
system of representation to question those production aspects. The importance
of the matter becomes obvious when one imagines the consequences of the mode
of production, the selectivity, the framing, and the impact of the film crew on the
'raw' material. These aspects are essentially inherent to the production of film.

Additionally, a film project is deeply rooted in an economical framework,
where decisions need to be taken for reasons of audience ratings, entertainment
qualities, funding, etc. When I was working as a documentary maker for the
National Television in Belgium, I once was asked to make a piece on immigrants in search of a home. Before I started, the editorial staff gave me a written
scenario in which the struggles of a veiled woman living with her ten children
in a small house were described. 'This is the family we need.' The experience
taught me that first a script is written down in order to guarantee funding, and
then a researcher is approached and assigned to find the character on display. In
other words, because of economic restrictions, the filmed reality needs to be
remodelled. As a result, documentary images are generally interpreted in a conventional way. These conventions are mainly based upon systems of belief of
dominant cultural groups. Political relations are reflected in those interpretations. Although the representational system is essentially a system of open
meanings, contextual interferences narrow the scope of interpretations into
stereotypes. The codes of representation are generally obscure constructions by
which cultural hegemony is maintained. Documentary reality can therefore
better be described as a site that constructs identities as opposed to representing them. In this sense, narratives dominate the reconstruction of the real:

> Rather, ethnography must redefine itself as that practice of representation that illu-
> minates the power of large-scale, imagined life possibilities over specific life trajec-
> tories. This is thickness with a difference, and the difference lies in a new alertness
> to the fact that ordinary lives today are more often powered not by the givenness of
> things but by the possibilities that the media (either directly or indirectly) suggest are
> available. (Appadurai 1996: 54)

Selection and Intrusion

Documentary film is, more than anything else, a matter of selection and intrusion. As a consequence of the selective nature of documentary making, and
thus of the time–space linearity of film, a certain type of narrative is developed
to guarantee the viewer the representational qualities of film. By means of this
type of narrating, 'reality' in film is supposedly being assured. Raoul Ruiz uses
the concept of a 'central conflict theory' to illuminate this idea. He defines it as
an all-encompassing narrative and dramatic guideline that is ruled by conflict
(Ruiz 1995: 14). He argues that the criteria according to which most of the
characters behave in today's films, documentaries etc. are drawn from one par-

ticular culture in which conflict is a pivotal idea. According to Ruiz, this theory has turned into a *predatory* theory, a system of ideas that devours and enslaves any other idea that might restrain its activity (ibid.: 15). Yet there is no strict equivalence between stories of conflict and everyday life. People fight and compete, but competition alone cannot contain the totality of the event that involves this.

Furthermore, he states that this theory yields a normative system. The products that comply with this norm have not only invaded the world but have also imposed their rules on most of the centres of audiovisual production across the planet, attempting to master the same logic of representation and practising the same narrative logic (Ruiz 1995: 21).

As a consequence of the 'intrusive' part of filmmaking, an exaggeration of performative behaviour can be ascertained. When a camera enters a room, certain types of acting or staging are being stimulated: a sort of amplified form of common behaviour. Moreover, it is as though the camera itself leads to a situation where not only the person in front of the camera but also the people behind it act in an almost programmed way. One of the students on our seminars wrote an entire thesis on the 'trap' a camera could be. Even with 'good intentions', lectures in visual anthropology and a good deal of common sense about what urban life might be, he found his own film 'trapped' into a stereotype. His conclusion was never to underestimate the power of a camera.

All these aspects constitute the mode of production, but are out of sight for the audience and the people who are represented. The essential elements of film are thus being covered up. When, why, and how selection and intrusion has taken place is being camouflaged by means of an Ancient Greek view on drama. By submitting the flow of experiences to the structure of a classical drama, one confides in a certain appropriation and an ideology-laden use of images. The viewer cannot locate censorship or accountability. Form (the type of narrative, the scenario) in and of itself thus carries a highly sophisticated ideological meaning. To ignore the mode of production of this form is to confine it in an ideological drama:

> What is presented as evidence remains evidence, whether the observing eye qualifies itself as being subjective or objective. At the core of such a rationale dwells, untouched, the Cartesian division between subject and object, that perpetuates a dualistic inside-versus-outside, mind-against-matter view of the world. Again, the emphasis is laid on the power of film to capture reality 'out there' for us 'in here'. The moment of appropriation and of consumption is either simply ignored or carefully rendered invisible according to rules of good and bad documentary. The art of talking-to-say-nothing goes hand-in-hand with the will to say, and to say only to confine something in a meaning. Truth has to be made vivid, interesting; it has to be 'dramatized' if it is to convince the audience of the evidence, whose 'confidence' in it allows truth to take shape. (Trinh 1990: 83)

Methodological Strategies

Introducing Seminars of Visual Anthropology

Six years ago Rik Pinxten of Ghent University, the documentary film department of Sint-Lukas (the School of Arts in Brussels) and I initiated a series of
workshops in visual anthropology. We assist students from both schools in the
production of documentaries on Belgian society. The interdisciplinary groups
comprise both anthropology and film students. In general, the workshop
explores the creative and critical use of cinema, focusing on the relation
between aesthetics and cultural politics in a practical and theoretical manner. It
challenges conventional notions of the mode of production, subjectivity, audience, and interpretation in relation to filmmaking, film viewing and the cine-
matic apparatus. Our main concern is to research avenues that may question
the accountability of images in a way relevant to the epistemology of visual representation. We argue that the mode of production of documentary images,
their format, adds meaning and alters interpretation. Individuals change their
behaviour to 'perform' for the camera – and for an imagined audience. Moreover, filmmakers use specific conventions and techniques – such as camera
angle, framing and editing – in representing the 'reality' that they are conveying.
These codes of representation form, in fact, an artificial representational system:

> The documentary can easily thus become a 'style': it no longer constitutes a mode of
> production or an attitude toward life, but proves to be only an element of aesthetics
> (or anti-aesthetics), which at best, and without acknowledging it, it tends to be in
> any case when, within, its own factual limits, it reduces itself to a mere category, or
> a set of persuasive techniques. Many of these techniques have become so 'natural' to
> the language of broadcast television that they go 'unnoticed.' (Trinh 1990: 88)

In the following, we propose some methodological strategies in developing a
critical and self-reflective space within visual systems, based on our empirical
experience.

Visual Diagnosis of Interaction

As Pinxten and Verstraete argue, identity construction is based on the interplay
of narratives and labels within a certain sociocultural context. Narratives are
constantly mobile through the dynamics caused by the intertwining of fact and
fiction, creating fluid identities: 'identity is performatively constituted by the
very "expressions" that are said to be its results' (Butler 1990: 25). In other
words, identity is a performance; it is what you *do* at particular times, rather
than a universal *who you are*. The concept of identity proposed is free-floating,
and not connected to an 'essence', it is instead thought of as a performance. The
construction of the self (of an individual, a group, a community and the like) is
also highly interlaced with the construction of selves in visual narratives. This
view on identity dynamics is fundamental in our visual anthropology seminars.

We developed some methods grounded in interactive research. Instead of
claiming the truth, we are researching the interaction of the research process
(Bourdieu 1980: Chap. 3). Ethnography is necessarily doublybiased (Pinxten

1997: 9). We conceive a 'fact' in ethnography as an item of knowledge usually expressed in a statement, which is, or can be, agreed upon by both the community of ethnographers and by the consultants of the culture concerned. The statement should be a true, correct or viable description of such cultural 'data' (Pinxten 1997: 9). This also holds for visual data. It is not the reality of the subjects that can be visualised, nor are we aiming at depicting our own ethnocentric interpretation either. It is the visual diagnosis of the interaction between researcher, subject and the impact of the system of representation that is searched for.

> Ethnographic films (which readily blur the boundaries between subjectivity and objectivity, observer and observed) address as their referent our relation to the historical present, usually the moment of filming. ... In viewing the scene in *Silverlake Life* when Tom Joslin lies dead and Mark Massi mourns his passing, the tremendous impact of such a moment lies, I believe, in the remains of an ethnographic referent that is not in the image, not in the visible evidence of death, not in the authentic location footage or in the historical moment now marked by it, but in the relation between all these aspects and the experiential moment of the encounter itself when this event unfolds again, not only as it was experienced at the time of filming by Mark Massi, and hence ethnographically, but also as it unfolds for the first time, for us. We experience the extraordinary indexical bond of history and the future we construct from it as they intertwine in the referential force field shaped in the present moment of historical consciousness. (Nichols 1994: xii)

It is the experience 'in-between' that is to be visualised. It is not the truth, nor the authenticity of the other that is being traced but the 'interval' as Trinh Minh-ha (1990: 96) describes it: 'Meaning can neither be imposed nor denied. Although every film is in itself a form of ordering and closing, each closure can defy its own closure, opening onto other closures, thereby emphasizing the interval between apertures and creating a space in which meaning remains fascinated by what escapes and exceeds it.'

In the year 2000 we were encouraged by the curator of 'Brussels 2000' Guido Minne to join a group called *Crossing Brussels*, organised by Eric Corijn of the Free University of Brussels (VUB) and funded by Brussels 2000. This group researched different public spaces in Brussels by means of three public buses. The buses were reorganised into an exposition space, a cinema and a café and parked in the researched public spaces in view of improving the collaboration between scientists and members of the community. The films produced by our students were shown in the bus located in the area where the films were made, in order to enhance the interaction and discussion of the production of the images. The preference for public buses was carefully thought out: the recognition and familiarity of these spaces lowered the gap between researcher and inhabitants. Also, the location of the buses 'on the spot' was perceived by the residents as a strong invitation to the lively discussions in the buses. The confrontation of students and their work with the residents lies at the heart of the engagement one needs to practise visual anthropology.

What we suggest as a methodological framework is a form of collaborative negotiation. An image can be perceived as a true image when participant and filmmaker share the meaning of this image (its truth). We do not expect more truthfulness or authenticity than this. If this image represents a recreation of the real which is agreed upon by researcher and participant, then we can assume that we evoke something of the interaction between them. As cited by Nichols: 'ethnographic film might, according to Stephen Tyler, respond to the call for evocation rather than representation in order to 'provoke an aesthetic integration that will have a therapeutic effect. It is, in a word, poetry."' (Nichols 1994: 82)

Fatimah Tobing Rony found interesting evidence in relation to *Nanook of the North* on how the lack of collaboration and negotiation created pertinent different perspectives on the film. The perception of the Inuit on the production of the film differed dramatically from the Western view. 'Recent research has shown that the Inuit found Flaherty and the filmmaking a source of great amusement, and this amusement may well account for Nanook's smile. The enigma of Nanook's smile allows the audience to project its own cultural presuppositions: from the point of view of an outsider he is childlike, from the Inuit point of view he may be seen as laughing at the camera' (Rony 1996: 111). Apparently, Nanook was having a good laugh when Flaherty tried to turn him into an actor performing 'a primitive man'. He was asked by Flaherty to wear clothes dated ten years ago, was asked to lick a gramophone, showing his ignorance of Western technology. 'Like a museum display in which sculpted models of family groups perform "traditional activities", Nanook's family adopts a variety of poses for the camera' (Rony 1996: 112). These acts all reinforced the image of a *primitive savage* the Western audience knew very well from exhibitions, zoos and museums. At that time, the Inuit were popular performers in those places, as they were treated as specimens and objects of curiosity (ibid.: 105).

In our workshop we encourage our students to develop a collaborative framework in their research in order to produce a film process that is appreciated by both parties, the researchers and the participants. The book that accompanies the documentaries contains photographs of the production process. The edition on the fishermen of Ostend three years ago presented a rectangular photo shot by one of the students showing the subjects of the film. This photo was presented next to a cubic photo that was taken by one of the subjects and showed the group of students. In this way, the form generated the representation of the maker, a more sophisticated way of revealing the production process.

Furthermore, to enhance this interactive view, the subjects of the workshops are chosen within subclasses of Belgian society. The reason for this type of research is also to identify the 'other' as part of the same culture in pointing out the differences-within-the-same. Projects include the multicultural experience in Genk (1999), the fisher community in Ostend (1998) and the First World War trauma in Vinkt (1997).

Formal Play

In our workshops we suggest looking upon the mode of production as a site of critique. Because of the previously elaborated reasons, we think it is crucial to include the production mode and responses to it in the film. In this way the

codes of representation are to be found in the film itself, therefore enhancing
the accessibility of the subject's image. I do not, however, want to imply an academic formalised system of feedback within the film. I prefer to consider it as a
formal play in which this type of self-reflection needs to find its own place in
the film. Or in other words: I believe it is necessary to explore artistically the
formal aspects of imagining cultural groups.

For example, when the film on Public Space in so-called Matonge, a neighbourhood in Brussels, was shown in the buses, the students were accused of
stereotyping the African community. These reactions were recorded on a mini-
disc player and used as a tool to deconstruct the original film in another editing.

This kind of formal playfulness was stimulated by the tradition in experimental filmmaking of the film school. In this tradition techniques of deconstruction and reconstruction in a plastic and textural way are elaborated.
Experimental filmmakers mostly work in an independent way. They refuse affiliation with the predominant modes of production, and they manage to organise their own circuits, their own festivals and most of all their own forms and
formats. A wide range of film and video makers, including Maya Deren, Peter
Kubelka, Jonas Mekas, Su Friedrich, Bill Viola, Kidlat Tahimik, Tracey Moffatt
and Chantal Akerman, are regarded as sources of inspiration here. Experimental film and ethnographic film have long been considered separate, autonomous
practices on the margins of mainstream cinema. Catherine Russell explores the
interplay between the two forms (Russell 1999).

Our workshops can be regarded as a play field within this intertwining of
traditions. We think it is important to open up this self-reflective and critical
stance to a playful and explorative mode. In our view, formal renewal challenges conventional modes of object–subject relationships, perception of audi-
ences, and content–form divisions. For instance, while researching the fisher
community in Ostend, the students came across a stereotypical and deep-
rooted expression: 'The fishermen are the Negroes of the city.' They used this
phrase as a tool to provoke reactions within the fisher community and in the
city of Ostend as a whole. In their documentary they assembled these recorded
phrases with photos in black and white of the people who were responding.
This process created a very strong image that deconstructed the stereotype but
nonetheless located its background.

Epilogue

The construction of identities in visuals plays a central role in imagining subjectivities. In this contribution I have tried to expand the theory on identity
dynamics developed by Pinxten and Verstraete by bringing in issues related to
identity construction in visual representations. By peeking over disciplinary
boundaries, abundantly citing authors from cultural studies, cognitive linguistics and film theory, and referring to the experience of the seminars in visual
anthropology at Ghent University and my own fieldwork, my aim was to take
up Appadurai's invitation to examine the relation between the 'word' and the

'world'. One avenue in this contribution explored the interlaced dynamics of the flow between fact and fiction in documentaries; one could name this 'the world'. Although a highly sophisticated mode of production fictionalises representation to a certain degree, the content of the images is mostly perceived as 'fact'. In questioning this, I have elaborated certain methodological strategies in documentary film production. In my view, at the heart of this flow between fact and fiction lies the inherent underspecification of images.

Another avenue therefore deals with the relation between the image and the word. Goodman and Elgin situate this underspecification as the main aspect of representational systems. By understanding the pictorial as an open token, the textual in documentaries is analysed as a way to reduce the complexity images can reveal. This reduction is intertwined with ideologies and political assumptions. In order to question this reduction of information, this stereotyping, I turned to cognitive linguists to elaborate on 'the word'. According to Fauconnier, Lakoff, Sweetser and Turner, both words and images induce mental spaces in the mind. Mental spaces are characterised by their space-building potential, thus mental-space constructions generally deal with a considerable amount of underspecification in the process of meaning construction. There are no precise indications of properties; they are negotiable in further elaborations during the communication. This view is a challenge for the analysis of identity dynamics in visual representation in as much as it invites an exploration of the dense and blurred relationship between images and texts used in visual representation.

Notes

1. Arjun Appadurai (1996: 49) 'There is an urgent need to focus on the cultural dynamics of what is now called deterritorialization. This term applies not only to obvious examples such as transnational corporations and money markets but also to ethnic groups, sectarian movements, and political formations, which increasingly operate in ways that transcend specific territorial boundaries and identities'.
2. 'British cultural studies situated culture within a theory of social production and reproduction, specifying the ways that cultural forms served either to further social control, or to enable people to resist. It analysed society as a hierarchical and antagonistic set of social relations characterized by the oppression of subordinate class, gender, race, ethnic, and national strata. Employing Gramsci's model of hegemony and counterhegemony, British cultural studies sought to analyse "hegemonic", or ruling, social and cultural forces of demonination and to seek "counterhegemonic" forces of resistance and contestation' (Durham and Kellner 2001: 16).
3. *Projection mappings* will project part of the structure of one domain onto another … the general (and deep) idea is that, in order to talk and think about some domains (*target* domains) we use the structure of other domains (*source* domains) and the corresponding vocabulary. Another important class of domain connections are the *pragmatic function mappings* … The two relevant domains, which may be set up locally, typically correspond to two categories of objects, which are mapped onto each other by a pragmatic function … A third class of mappings, *schema mappings,* operate when a general schema, frame, or model is used to structure a situation in context' (Fauconnier 1997: 9–11).
4. My thanks go to Eve Sweetser, who offered this insight through our conversations on the subject.

5. Conceptual blending presents a clarification for perceiving represented or filmed reality as the real: the content of those images is frame-blended with the form whereby the form only induces the cognition of the 'real', whether or not the form is actually factual. The typical documentary techniques then are blended with their 'original' content, which was claiming to reveal reality 'as it really happened'. (Again, thanks to Eve Sweetser.)

Bibliography

Appadurai, Arjun. 1996. *Modernity at Large: Cultural Dimensions of Globalization. Public Worlds. Vol. 1*. Minneapolis and London: University of Minnesota Press.

Bourdieu, Pierre. 1980. *Le sens pratique*. Paris: Edition de Minuit.

Butler, Judith. 1990. *Gender Trouble: Feminism and the Subversion of Identity*. London and New York: Routledge.

Chow, Rey. 1995. *Primitive Passions*. New York: Columbia University Press.

Fauconnier, Gilles, Lakoff, George and Sweetser, Eve 1994. Mental Spaces: Aspects of Meaning Construction in Natural Language. Cambridge University Press.

———— 1997. *Mappings in Thought and Language*. Cambridge: Cambridge University Press.

———— and Turner, Mark. 1999. 'A Mechanism of Creativity', *Poetics Today*, Vol. 20, No. 3: 397–418.

Goodman, Nelson and Elgin, Catherine. 1988. *Reconceptions in Philosophy and Other Arts and Sciences*. London: Hackett Publishing Co.

Durham, Meenakshi Gigi and Kellner, Douglas (eds.) 2000. *Media and Cultural Studies: Keyworks (Keyworks in Cultural Studies)*. London: Blackwell Publishers.

Narayan, Shweta. 2000. 'Mappings in Art and Language: Conceptual Mappings in Neil Gaiman's Sandman'. Unpublished Senior Honours Thesis in Cognitive Science, UC Berkeley.

Nichols, Bill. 1994. *Blurred Boundaries: Questions in Meaning in Contemporary Culture*. Bloomington and Indianapolis: Indiana University Press.

Pink, Sarah. 2001. *Doing Visual Ethnography: Images, Media and Representations in Research*. London: Sage Publications.

Pinxten, Rik. 1997. *When the Day Breaks. Essays in Anthropology and Philosophy*. Frankfurt-am-Main, Berlin, Bern, New York, Paris and Vienna: Peter Lang.

Rony, Fatimah Toby. 1996. *The Third Eye: Race, Cinema and Ethnographic Spectacle*. Durham, NC: Duke University Press.

Rose, Gilian. 2001. *Visual Methodologies: An Introduction to Interpreting Visual Objects*. London: Sage Publications.

Ruiz, Raul. 1995. *Poetics of Cinema*. New York: Distributed Art Publishers.

Russell, Catherine. 1999. *Experimental Ethnography: The Work of Film in the Age of Video*. Durham, NC: Duke University Press.

Talmy, Leonard. 1995. 'Fictive Motion in Language and "ception"'. In *Language and Space*, eds. Paul Bloom, Marie Peterson, Lynn Nadel and Merrill Garrett. Cambridge, Mass: MIT Press.

Trinh, Minh-ha. 1990. 'Documentary Is/Not a Name', *October* 52, Spring: 76–100.

NOTES ON CONTRIBUTORS

Koen De Munter studied Romanic Languages and Comparative Science of Culture at Ghent University. On the basis of fieldwork with the urban Aymara in El Alto (Bolivia) from 1995 to 2000, for his doctoral thesis he researched philosophical-anthropological questions in studying indigenous pro-gression in the Andes, using concepts such as 'cultural intuitions' and 'cultural tides' (*Indigenous progression in the Andes*, 2003). He is currently a postdoctoral assistant at Ghent University and teaches courses in cultural anthropology and anthropological approaches towards postcoloniality.

Chia Longman is a Postdoctoral Fellow of the Fund for Scientific Research –Flanders, affiliated with the Department of Comparative Sciences of Culture at Ghent University. Her doctoral thesis focused on theoretical and methodological issues in the study of gender and religion from a comparative social science perspective, including a case study on religious identity among strictly Orthodox Jewish women in Antwerp. Her current research concerns religious feminism in multicultural contexts, particularly modern Orthodox Jewish women's religious activism. She teaches courses in gender studies and history of anthropological theories. Longman has published various articles, including 'Empowering and Engendering "Religion": A Critical Perspective on Ethnographic Holism', in *Social Anthropology* (2002).

Lieve Orye is a Postdoctoral Fellow of the Fund for Scientific Research, working at the Department of Comparative Sciences of Culture at Ghent University. Her research consists mainly in an analysis of fundamental methodological and meta-theoretical discussions within the study of religion, which is considered as a cultural phenomenon. Orye published a book on a section of her doctoral research entitled *Verborgen hypotheses in menswetenschap: een analyse van drie visies op religiestudies* (Hidden Hypotheses in Human Sciences: An Analysis of Three Perspectives on Religious Studies) in 2001, as well as several articles, including '"It's about Us" Religious Studies as Human Science', in *Method and Theory in the Study of Religion* (2001).

Rik Pinxten is Professor of Anthropology and head of the Department of Comparative Sciences of Culture at Ghent University. He has published widely and internationally on the anthropology of knowledge and the comparative study of religion. His fieldwork expertise has concentrated on the Navajo Indians (U.S.) and minority communities in Flanders (Belgium). He recently organised two international conferences on racism, of which the proceedings were published in *Europe's New Racism? Causes, Manifestations and Solutions*, an earlier volume in this series (2002).

An van Dienderen studied Art History, Comparative Science of Culture and Audio-Visual Arts. She has made several documentaries, among which is the poetic documentary *Nachtelijke Bezoekers* (Visitors of the Night) (1998) on the matriarchal society of Mosuo women in the province of Yunnan, China. With Didier Volckaert she produced and directed *Tu ne verras pas Verapaz*, released in 2002. The film elaborates on the history of the (Belgian) colonisation of Santo Tomas de Castilla in Guatemala, in 1843, and searches for descendants in Guatemala; the film is linked to themes such as migration, cultural identity and the green grass of home. van Dienderen regularly gives lectures and workshops on visual anthropology, and is preparing a PhD in visual anthropology at Ghent University.

Ghislain Verstraete is a sociocultural worker, graduate in Comparative Science of Culture and was a visiting scholar at Syracuse University (NY). He is a researcher at the Centre for Intercultural Communication and Interaction (CICI) at Ghent University, working in the area of the problems and conflicts arising from multicultural society, on which he is also currently finishing his doctoral thesis. Verstraete has conducted fieldwork in Europe, the U.S., and South Africa. Together with Rik Pinxten he edited the book *Cultuur en macht* (Culture and Power) (1998), and has written various articles on interculturalism in the welfare sector.

INDEX